The Alternative Worship Primer

Revised and Expanded

Cindy Hollenberg

A LifeQuest Publication

The Alternative Worship Primer

Revised and Expanded

Cindy Hollenberg

This book is dedicated to Steve Clapp, who has mentored me and encouraged me to pursue my goals, and who has generously offered his own talents and gifts to this project. Thank you. You are a true friend.

Copyright © 2003 by LifeQuest.

All rights reserved. No portion of this book may be reproduced in any form or by any process or technique without the written consent of the publisher, except for brief quotations embodied in critical articles or reviews.

For further information, contact: LifeQuest, 6404 S. Calhoun Street, Fort Wayne, Indiana 46807. 260-744-6510. DadofTia@aol.com

Biblical quotations, unless otherwise noted, are from the New Revised Standard Version of the Bible, copyrighted 1989 by the Division of Christian Education, National Council of Churches, and are used by permission. This book contains sample surveys for local church use. You may reproduce any of these or modify them for your congregation or membership group.

Thanks to Kristen Leverton Helbert, Stacey Sellers, and the staff of Evangel Press for their work on this project.

Cover art © Jantina Eshleman.

ISBN 1-893270-19-X

Manufactured in the United States of America

Contents

INTRODUCTION 5

Part I–THE BASICS

Chapter 1	What is alternative worship?	7
Chapter 2	How does alternative worship differ from traditional worship?	10
Chapter 3	Why do people want alternative worship?	25
Chapter 4	Who wants alternative worship?	27
Chapter 5	Will some people resist alternative worship?	31
Chapter 6	Why should we consider offering alternative worship?	33

Part II–DO YOUR HOMEWORK

Chapter 7	Do we need alternative worship?	35
Chapter 8	What should we include in our worship surveys?	45
Chapter 9	Should we have separate services, blended services, or alternating services?	48
Chapter 10	Who should be involved in the planning process?	53
Chapter 11	How do we handle opposition to alternative worship?	55
Chapter 12	How do we promote an alternative service?	61
Chapter 13	What other resources will we need?	67

Part III–TEST TIME!

Chapter 14 How can we integrate more alternative experiences into our existing worship service(s)? 71

Chapter 15 How involved should the minister be in the service? 73

Chapter 16 Where can we find music and musicians appropriate for an alternative worship service? 74

Chapter 17 How do we define success with alternative worship? 76

Chapter 18 What other resources are available? 79

Chapter 19 What do copyright laws really say? 82

Part IV–GRADUATION

Chapter 20 So, may we review please? 84

Chapter 21 What notes may we take with us? 88

Chapter 22 Any final hints? 96

Introduction

Worship is changing! More and more congregations are starting new worship services that are contemporary or alternative. Other churches are seeking to blend both traditional and alternative elements in the same service. Many churches want to increase their use of alternative worship styles but are unsure how to proceed. The purpose of this book is to help:

- Leaders who have not started an alternative service or a blended service and want guidance in that process.

- Leaders who are already working with a contemporary or alternative service and would like to improve their results.

- Leaders who are already working with a blended service but recognize the need to increase the proportion of contemporary or alternative experiences which are part of that service.

- Leaders who want to maximize the outreach potential of their worship experiences.

This book focuses on alternative or contemporary worship elements because that is the best way to help both those working with separate alternative services and those working with blended services. The assumption is that readers are already familiar with the elements of traditional worship services.

Alternative or contemporary worship may seem daunting or mysterious. It may fill a pastor and other leaders with fear, or it may be just another item on a long "to do" list. For whatever reason, those of you reading this book have asked for help. And while no book can cover every detail of what your particular church will experience in the process, this book will give you the basics of what you need to do and how to go about doing it.

This book is called a primer because it is a simple, easy-to-follow book which gives the first principles necessary to comprehend the subject of alternative worship. With this book as a foundation, you should feel more confident with innovation in worship. As you gain more experience of your own, you will move ahead in confidence of God's creative spirit within you. . . and within those you choose to involve in the process!

The process of planning, promoting and leading alternative worship does not need to be mysterious. Just as you learned to create traditional worship services and to determine needs for ministry in other areas of church life, so too can you learn to create and use alternative worship services. Creating alternative worship, if taken one step at a time, can be a very rewarding experience. May you enjoy the journey!

Part I–The Basics

Even if you already are working with alternative worship, either as part of a separate service or a blended service, you'll find this review of the basics helpful.

Chapter One: What is alternative worship?

Alternative worship is sometimes referred to as contemporary, experimental, or nontraditional worship. It is a worship experience which is different from the traditional worship service of hymns, prayers, a sermon or homily, and a benediction. In general, the alternative experience offers less structure, more creative approaches to "getting the message out," and a greater variety of music and other performing art forms.

Alternative worship may be big or small, quiet and reflective, or loud and upbeat. It may be interactive or totally nonparticipative. As a general rule, there are no rules! Although this is, of course, an oversimplification, alternative worship can truly be whatever your imagination and your inspiration might create. You might even create a service which is quite alternative in nature by having an entire worship service focused on traditional hymns.

What is important here is mainly the structure. Consider your own worship services by looking over the bulletins or handouts from the last several weeks. Do you almost always open with a prayer or a Call to Worship? Is this usually followed by congregational sharing? Is there a pattern to where hymns and Scripture readings are placed? Have there been only rare occasions in which a sermon or homily is not utilized? Is it unusual for there to be no choral anthem from the choir? Does the closing of the service (benediction, closing prayer, closing hymn, passing the peace, etc.) follow a pattern?

If you answered "yes" to all (or almost all) of the above questions, your services would probably be classified as traditional. Even if you have contemporary music at times, the structure is still mainly traditional. It doesn't change very much. People can count on it. Many, including yourself perhaps, are comfortable with it. And there's nothing wrong with that . . . if the services are meeting the worship needs of those to whom you minister.

The Alternative Worship Primer

If you answered "no" to more than one question, but "yes" to most of them, you already offer at least some element of nontraditional worship. Perhaps you change the structure every once in a while, opting to offer a drama rather than a sermon. Perhaps you vary the structure–or at least the order of worship–every few services. Perhaps you add in other elements to your service, such as liturgical dance, Scriptural dialogue, or videos. If so, you are probably somewhat familiar with alternative forms of worship. Your services may best be described as "blended." You at the least offer elements of alternative worship in some of your services. Hopefully, you have had a positive response to these offerings.

So, what do less traditional services look like? Consider the following examples (from *Alternatives for Worship*, Hollenberg Snider and Clapp).

A. A Service on Tithing and Stewardship

The service opens with an actor/actress playing the part of a young child who has just received a dollar and doesn't want to share it. Next, two readers juxtapose the Zacchaeus story with our own tendencies to be selfish and our rationalizing in order to do that. A Scripture reading follows. After that, a tongue-in-cheek drama is presented which mimics a self-help meeting–only this meeting is for people who make excuses! The service closes with another Scripture passage, followed by a short prayer and a contemporary song.

B. A Service on AIDS and Grief

This service is divided into four parts: Life, Sickness, Death, and New Life. It includes a series of letters to parents from a daughter who has somehow contracted AIDS. Interspersed between letters the worshipers sing the verses of "Amazing Grace." The opening of the service is a reading based on Psalm 23, after which there is a story for children. The service includes a candle-lighting ceremony and closing response from the worship participants.

The Basics

C. A Service on God's Provision and the Role of Food in Our Lives

This service begins with the singing of a contemporary hymn, followed by Scripture. A short reflection on manna from the worship leader is offered. After this, worship participants are invited to eat! Another short reflection is offered on Jesus' eagerness to feed those to whom he ministered. The service closes with a prayer and a song. But wait! The real ending is in the food offered in fellowship as people leave the meeting place!

D. A Service on Dreams and Visions

This service opens with secular music from the movie *Titanic*, of which a clip is shown later in the service. It includes a Scripture reading, a litany, two songs and a mini-sermon on dreams. The video clip is used to underscore the message in the mini-sermon. A short prayer follows the video clip.

E. A Service on Discrimination and Exclusion

This service opens with a short Reader's Theater, followed by the first verse of a noncontemporary, but "out of season" hymn. After that, we hear from three different people, each telling of their particular experiences with discrimination or exclusion. Another verse of the hymn, another three people. Another verse, another three people. Another verse, and now the voice of Jesus (Scripture). A final verse, followed by a parting familiar voice.

These are only a few of the variations for alternative worship services. There are many possibilities and permutations. As you can see, there is not a set structure to the services, although many open and close in a similar fashion–either with a prayer or a closing song. You will need to decide what seems most appropriate for those who worship in your church, keeping in mind your own comfort level. Other differences between traditional and nontraditional worship will be explored in the next chapter.

Chapter Two: How does alternative worship differ from traditional worship?

Many people attending an alternative worship service will have at least a general idea of what to expect–and what not to expect–in the service. They will probably expect to hear music that is more contemporary. They may expect to see drama, video, storytelling, puppets, clowns, and other media in place of the sermon. They may also expect to hear a more challenging mix of messages–a mix which may include more controversial topics, from which traditional services often shy away. And they will probably expect a more casual atmosphere than what is usually found in a traditional service.

Those of us who grew up in the church often take many of the traditions of worship for granted. We assume that the pastor will give a sermon from the pulpit. We assume the service will last an hour (or more). We assume the worshipers will all sit in the pews in the sanctuary. We assume that everyone knows what an anthem is or what *benediction* means. We assume that people will come to the service dressed for . . . well . . . dressed for church!

There are a large number of people, however, to whom church feels foreign. Whether they are simply unfamiliar or have been previously alienated, some people are not comfortable with those very things that we may take for granted. Even if these people are your next door neighbors, it may be as though they live in another culture. They do not know the language. They do not know what to do when. They may have only a vague idea of what church is. So while some people may have very definite expectations, another group of people may have no idea what to expect. For these people, worship experiences need to be able to connect them personally with the wonder of the living, breathing, loving God.

This does not mean that traditional worship cannot make this connection. What this means is that alternative worship may achieve this goal more easily. We can think of traditional worship as more ritualized and hierarchical. In contrast, alternative worship is often more casual and free. In short, contemporary worship is more accessible to a wider variety of people.

The Basics

More specifically, alternative worship differs from traditional worship in language, music, message media, length of service, attire worn, physical arrangement, and issues raised. I will tackle these in the order given.

A. Language

The language in an alternative worship service is often very different from traditional service language. Alternative worship tends to shy away from "churchy language." Words such as *majesty* and *glory* have less meaning in a society which does not have a king or queen. This doesn't mean that you can never use these words; just be careful how often you use them. And when you do use them, you may want to consider providing a biblical or theological context. Words like *justification*, *sanctification*, *redemption*, and *incarnation* need explanation for people who did not grow up in the church. These cautions, in fact, apply to traditional services as well.

You may also find that some of the words we use to describe Jesus, such as Lord and Master, may either be meaningless or have negative connotations for some people. The words *Lord* and *Master* may even bring up images of slavery or dominance/submission paradigms, whether conscious or not. Consider an African American whose family history contains stories of his ancestors' struggles against slavery. Consider a young woman who has recently emerged from an abusive, controlling relationship and who is working extremely hard at never allowing herself to be dominated again. You may have people not accustomed to these words fighting an inner rebellion simply from hearing them. Providing the biblical or theological context of such words becomes important.

Beyond this, worshipers who want a truly alternative experience may be uncomfortable with traditional worship words such as *sermon*, *litany*, *anthem*, *hymn*, *offering*, and *benediction*. The unchurched (or church shy) person may ask: What are those things anyway? Why can't they call a song a song? Many alternative services choose to say *song* rather than *hymn*, *opening music* rather than *prelude*, *opening prayer* rather than *invocation*, *closing prayer* rather than *benediction*, and *closing music* rather than *postlude*. Again, remember that not everyone grew up in the church and became gradually accustomed to its unique language.

The Alternative Worship Primer

Speaking further on language, use of nongendered, culturally sensitive language is important for many who did not grow up in the church. Try not to refer to God only as Father, but also as Mother. We need not limit our images of God to a few masculine descriptions.

Some people in our society may initially feel uncomfortable hearing God referred to in feminine terms. Because many of us have grown up in congregations in which God was routinely referred to with masculine language, it may take time for us to feel comfortable with more inclusive language. People who did not grow up in the church and people who are unhappy with traditional worship, however, will respond very positively to the inclusion of feminine references to God. The Bible clearly asserts that we are ALL made in God's image. It's important that our ways of talking about God not exclude those who are female. This is especially important if you want to effectively speak to and reach young adults.

All of the cautions about language also apply to the music. Most traditional hymns–as well as much of contemporary Christian music–use either gendered language or traditional references (Lord, Master). It is actually quite difficult to find songs which do not. But you have options! You might preface the singing with "permission" to change wording which may feel uncomfortable to individuals. Perhaps a better choice, however, is to change to words for the singers.

If you decide to change the words, you will want to present the songs or hymns the way you want them sung. You may choose to hand out song sheets, or include the song/hymn words in the service handout. If you are blessed with computer savvy technicians, you can offer words on a screen, using computers and programs like PowerPoint™. (Note: It is an infringement of copyright laws to purchase one copy and "distribute" it by computer or photocopying. This is only an option if you have purchased enough copies for the entire gathering. See Chapter 19 for a further discussion on copyright laws.)

Stories and examples should include and expand upon the experiences of women from the Bible and from contemporary times as well as the experiences of men. For example, discussion of the story of David and Bathsheba almost always focuses exclusively on David. But that is only half the story. What

The Basics

about Bathsheba? What must she have felt? How did she come to terms with her grief? Did she ever learn to love David? What was her faith?

In the same manner, resist the temptation to dichotomize men and women. For example, historically men have been referred to as rational and spiritual while women have been thought of as irrational and sensual. Since traditional Christian thought is that spirituality is higher than sensuality, by extension men have been thought of by some–even if only subconsciously–as closer to God than women. The message may be subtle, but it is nevertheless clear. Many women of today are sensitive to it.

Likewise, watch out for ethnocentric paradigms. For those of us of European descent, we have traditionally pictured Jesus as light skinned, perhaps having blue eyes. But this is, of course, highly unlikely! Think about what part of the world Jesus came from. He probably looked at least more Arabic or possibly African than European! Our image of Jesus, like our image of God, says a lot about how we think about the world. Further, keep in mind that the Bible has historically been used by misguided persons to justify the horrors of slavery, the nightmare of the Holocaust, the slaughter and torture of indigenous cultures, and the eradication of opposing religions. The Bible, and other church teachings, can be a wellspring of truth and joy, but they can also be the source of misery and pain when used thoughtlessly.

B. Music

Another difference between alternative and traditional worship services is the music. Choose a variety of music. While some people believe that you should only use contemporary songs in an alternative service, I would say that if you want to use a hymn in a service, go ahead. Just don't rely solely on traditional hymns week after week. There is much more out there! Although you may opt for traditional hymns at times, you may also want to consider contemporized versions of those hymns. Many Christian singers, such as Amy Grant or Michael W. Smith, offer traditional hymns sung in a more contemporary style.

I would also suggest using the organ only rarely . . . or not at all. Many hymns sound just as beautiful when accompanied by piano or guitar, or sung a cappella. You may want to use–if you are so blessed–a variety of instruments to accompany singing: piano, electronic keyboard, guitar, or hammered dulcimer, to name a few. Consider adding drums, trumpets, xylophone, harp, maracas, harpsichord, bells, hand chimes, banjo, ukulele, steel pan, saxophone, or any other instrument you have available. Use of more contemporary instruments to accompany even traditional hymns will make the music feel contemporary. Soloists or small groups of singers may wish to use accompaniment tapes.

The key to choosing music is variety. Either within a service or within a series of services, choose music and musical styles to fit the "mood" of the service. Praise music, while perfectly appropriate for services which celebrate the love of God, may not fit well with a service about child abuse or learning how to grieve. There are some hymns which may speak to issues of prejudice, but you may also find something appropriate in contemporary Christian–or even secular–music.

You may want to invite a band or choral group to perform, either for variety, or because you don't have enough people in your own congregation who can do contemporary music. Often, local high school groups are available for performances either for a small fee or for a donation. Consider adding in some purely instrumental music in some services. Consider solos on piano, flute, guitar, or other instruments. Consider duets, trios, and quartets as well.

Sometimes, you may want to opt for prerecorded music rather than having a live performance. I would caution you, however, to limit this type of music, as people generally prefer to see the musician(s) perform. Try to get live talent whenever feasible. There may be times, however, when prerecorded music is preferable. This might include times when you want music only for background, or when you want the worshipers to meditate inwardly over music. Also, prerecorded music often works well as worshipers are gathering or as they are leaving the meeting place.

Consider at times adding interpretive or liturgical dance when you use prerecorded music. This gives the worshipers something to watch and adds a visual message to the auditory one. Large churches may have their own liturgical dance group, or may want to start one. Small churches, if there is no one skilled in

The Basics

dance, may want to contact larger churches or dance collectives to find out about local talent. Some churches which have historically opposed dancing may want to offer some explanation on the history and symbolism of liturgical dance. You may even want to consider training workshops if the response to dance is favorable.

Again, the key to the music is variety. Although you don't want to vary the music ONLY for variety's sake, alternative means different. Don't get stuck in a rut. There is a huge selection of music just waiting to be discovered!

C. Message Media

Alternative services communicate the message in varied, creative ways. One of the biggest complaints that people have about traditional worship services is that the sermons are boring. The reality is that people simply have shorter attention spans than they used to, thanks to our mass-media, sound-byte, electronic culture. But another reason many people don't like sermons is that they don't like lectures of any form. For some, this may stem from subconscious unresolved parent/child issues. For others, a sermon (which to them is a lecture) doesn't feel like worship. It simply feels like being forced to listen to a textbook on God. And there's no "stop" button!

For those churches who choose to "blend" services, offering some alternative elements along with the traditional, you will probably have sermons some of the time. When planning time permits, you might consider rewriting the sermon so that it feels less traditional. Consider the following possibilities:

- Have a "devil's advocate" respond to the teaching, challenging the sermonizer to probe the subject more deeply or from a different perspective. This may be in the form of a one-time interruption or an ongoing conversation.

- Set up a "conversation" whereby two (or more) people contribute to the understanding of the issue at hand.

- Solicit questions, comments, etc. from the worshipers. Make the sermon more interactive.

The Alternative Worship Primer

- Simply add another person. The second person may be the illustrator, using anecdotal stories to highlight the point(s) just made by the person giving the sermon. Or she and the pastor may alternate speaking at appropriate points in the sermon. Just make sure those points make sense!

- Shorten the sermon. Perhaps you'll want to call it something else (like a meditation, or a reflection). Resist the temptation to share all that you know on a topic in a single message. Divide a sermon into three mini-sermons, spread over three weeks. Or, spread the sermon out over the length of the service. Who says the sermon has to come all at once?

- Try to tell the sermon in more of a storytelling format. Just as novels often affect us at a very deep emotional level, so too can storytelling. Effective storytelling may be the most powerful form of preaching.

These are just a few of the ways sermons can be rewritten to seem less formal, less traditional. You will need to decide whether or not to keep the "sermon" label. There may be people who object to the use of that term. There may be people who object to anything that is NOT labeled such! And there is even a possibility that, if you do it well enough, people who used to groan (at least inwardly) at sermon time, will learn to enjoy it!

There are many other possibilities for communicating the message of the service. Sometimes these will replace the traditional sermon. A few of these possibilities follow:

1. **Drama**–Dramas or skits are often effective in communicating messages in worship, especially if the drama can present some kind of dilemma between opposing characters. These dramas may be humorous, pointing out the ironies of life, or highlighting the quirks of human nature. They may be quite serious, drawing the audience into the depths of the characters' struggles in life. Some of the best dramas use both humor and tragedy to make a point. One of the most effective techniques in storytelling or drama is to keep the audience laughing (or at least chuckling) until the very end when the reality of the problem hits home. Keep

The Basics

in mind that dramas take time in order to be effective. Plan ahead. Choose (or write) the drama and cast the players well in advance. Give the players time to learn their parts and rehearse so that it flows smoothly. Bad drama presentations will be remembered at least as well as good ones!

2. **Video clips**–There are lots of movies which have very poignant scenes which, when used in a worship service, can illustrate particular points. Chapter 18 offers a few suggestions from movies which might fit certain message themes.

   It is important to "set the scene" when using video clips. Presumably, you have talked about a particular point. Once you have outlined that point, say to the worshipers something like, "What you are about to see is a short scene from the movie *(title)*. In this scene, *(character name)* has just *(done whatever is important to your point)*. Let's see what happens."

   Keep the segment short, probably between five and ten minutes. You're only using the segment–the clip–to illustrate a point, not to entertain an audience. Besides, if you show too much of a movie to a large group of people, copyright laws begin to be problematic. I'll have more to say later about copyright laws.

   Set up the video equipment and segments ahead of time. Make sure screens are large enough–and that there are enough of them–so that the entire audience can see well. Adjust the volume ahead of time. And forward the video to the appropriate selection. If you will be showing more than one clip, have another person ready to quietly switch the tapes or DVDs after the first one.

3. **Series of short reflections interspersed with music**– As in the example B (Service on AIDS and Grief) from the previous chapter, this is a very effective way to communicate the service message. The series may be several related stories or readings, a time-lapse series (as in the example given), a series of similar thoughts from differing perspectives, or simply a longer reflection (or variation on a sermon) broken up. It is usually best to

use the same music throughout so that the service itself doesn't feel broken up. Singing different verses of the same hymn or song after each segment is a good way to bind the various pieces together.

4. **Dialogue**–You may want to write a dialogue between two biblical characters, especially if there is an element of tension between them. Again, using David and Bathsheba as an example, wouldn't it be interesting to create an imaginary but possible dialogue between them when Bathsheba learns that David had her husband killed?

   Another option for dialogue is to create a conversation between a biblical character and a contemporary person. How might their perspectives differ? What can each teach the other?

   And of course, you can create a dialogue between two contemporary persons, between a person and her conscience, between Mother Nature and a manufacturing executive, between an abuser and a victim. The list is nearly endless. Just put your imagination to work!

5. **Reader's Theater**–Unless you're familiar with Reader's Theater, this may the most difficult type of media to write. Reader's Theater is basically a carefully arranged song . . . without the music! It usually tells a story, but beyond that it is actually orchestrated for maximum impact. Sometimes lines are read solo, other times duo or trio or even chorus. There may be chants going on in the background. There may be a back and forth movement from one group of readers to another. It's a very powerful experience if done well. But like drama, it can fall flat if it's not.

6. **Symbolic Interaction**–This category includes such things as eating and drinking, building something such as an altar, tearing something down such as a wall, embracing and speaking with persons near you, carrying items such as rocks, planting seeds or trees, washing your hands or another's feet, lighting candles in remembrance of someone or something, and anointing for spiritual healing. When these interactions (and

The Basics

others) are used with explanations as to their symbolism, they can be very powerful, moving experiences. Sometimes you will want only worship leaders to actually do the action, but most times you will want to instruct the worshipers and have them involved.

7. **Guided Meditations**–This option should probably be used rather sparingly, unless your particular set of worshipers is comfortable with protracted times of meditation. Usually, the worship leader suggests a place for worshipers to "go" in their minds: a place of peace, a place of rest, etc. Leave it up to the worshipers to imagine their own peaceful, restful place. For some it will be the woods. For others it will be the ocean. For still others it will be in a favorite chair. The key is to give time for every person to actually envision themselves there. After that, you will want them to picture something else in their minds. Then something else, then perhaps one more thing. Each time, allow time between whatever instructions you give. And don't ask them to do too much. Four good "envisionings" is fairly hard work! As an example, one guided meditation might be as follows:

- "Close your eyes and take three deep, calming breaths. Allow yourself to travel to a place that puts your heart at peace. Look around you. Listen to the silence and the sounds of that place. Let the peace enter you." (pause)

- "Imagine now that God is approaching you. God is smiling at you, with arms outstretched to hold you. Imagine resting your head on God's shoulder and being enfolded in God's arms." (pause)

- "Now envision Christ holding both of your hands, looking deeply into your eyes, telling you that you are made in God's image. God is breathing into you the strength to face whatever trials may come your way this week." (pause)

- "Breathe in the power of God. Revel in the warmth and comfort God offers. See yourself as part of the divine plan on earth. And when you are ready to return, open your eyes." (pause)

8. **Storytelling**–We are never too old to enjoy a good story, especially when told from memory by someone who is able to captivate the listeners and carry them into the story itself. Stories may be written by you or someone you know, they may be gleaned from books, they may come straight from the Bible. Stories usually include getting to know at least one character, some sort of conflict to be resolved, and a unique occurrence that offers insight on the solution. Stories may be from biblical times or the present day. They may be very close to home or geographically far away. They may be rooted in reality or totally fantastic. Basically, they can be anything you want them to be!

9. **Series of songs with short reflections on each**–One idea that I've used which works especially well with youth is to have each youth (or a select few if you have a very large group) choose a song which he or she would like to have the worshipers hear. Have the teens write short meditations or reflections on what the songs mean to them. In the service, the songs are either performed or played with the youth introducing the song, then sharing their reflection afterward. Even songs which some church members dislike may be seen in a different light when spoken about with passion by a young person!

As you can see from the above list, there are many possibilities for alternative worship. The key is variety. Do not do the same thing every time. Be creative! You are only limited by your imagination and your inspiration.

D. Length of Service

In general, alternative services are shorter than traditional services. Often alternative worship is embraced by younger people. These younger people have grown up in an era of fast-moving images, of sound bytes, of computers and videos, and action-adventure themes. They do not want to sit still for an hour.

The Basics

A good goal is forty minutes. That way, if your service runs up to ten minutes either short or long, you're still offering a worship experience between thirty and fifty minutes. Most people prefer shorter services rather than longer ones. However, if a person travels ten or more minutes each way to a service, and the service only lasts twenty minutes, he or she may feel that the experience was not worth the effort.

You may be familiar with some churches which have worship services that last ninety minutes or even two hours. These are usually churches which utilize teaching sermons and have a very fast-paced service. It requires truly exceptional preaching to hold the interest of a congregation for more than twenty minutes, and the music and drama must also be exceptional if the service is more than an hour in length. Most churches, especially those wanting to reach youth and young adults, will create shorter services.

In general, your message ought to be able to be communicated, without the extras that enhance the message, in twenty minutes. If you can't do this, perhaps you need to narrow your focus. Dispense with anything that doesn't add to the goals of the service.

Pay attention to time! No matter how good your service may be, if it goes longer than most people think it should be, they won't hear a thing after they think it should be over!

E. Attire Worn

Alternative worship is more casual than traditional worship, and your clothes should show it. Have worship leaders dress comfortably and encourage worshipers to do so as well. One complaint heard over and over again, especially by younger people, but also by those who have less money, is that church should not be a fashion contest. Nor should we be sending the message that you have to dress up in order to honor God. Jesus didn't!

Those who are attracted to alternative worship experiences are usually also the ones who enjoy dressing casually. If they come to a service dressed in jeans and a sweater, and see everyone else in suits and ties or dresses, they will not feel like they fit in. They will wonder whether this service is really so different after all. They may not come back.

The Alternative Worship Primer

F. Physical Arrangement

Alternative worship often looks different than a traditional church service. Remember that you are worshiping with people who for one reason or another, prefer something different. So the physical arrangement of the room and even the room used might look different. This may be not be possible for very well attended services. If the only possibility is for people to sit in pews in the sanctuary, by all means go ahead.

If you do not use the sanctuary, you are free to arrange the room any way you like. You might set up chairs in a circle, or in small groups of four or five facing each other. You may decide that rows will work best for some services, while sitting around tables works best for another service. If you have a small group of people and the service calls for an intimate setting, arrange the room to maximize this and place yourself (if you are the worship leader) in a relational position rather than a hierarchical one (i.e. on the same level, rather than above). If the service is celebrating the beauty of creation, hold the service outside or perhaps in front of a large window with a great view.

And what about the worship leader(s)? Even if you are in a sanctuary, the pastor or worship leader does not have to speak from the pulpit. He or she can circulate through the room or can sit on a tall stool near the front. Examine your particular service and look at the size and make-up of your group.

G. Issues Raised

Often, alternative worship boldly goes where no traditional service wants to go: controversy. At least some of the time. Many people attracted to alternative worship are well aware, either from personal experience or vicariously through the experiences of family and friends, that life offers some very difficult situations and choices. While these situations and choices are often not pleasant to deal with, religious faith can make a huge difference in how a person handles them.

Typically, services which address controversial issues are the most difficult to create. This is because we often do not know exactly where we stand on some issues and because we are afraid to confront the fears and prejudices of ourselves and of

The Basics

others. Consider such issues as economic exploitation, rape, complacency in the face of injustice, racial discrimination, child abuse, spouse abuse, governmental corruption, corruption in the church, the injustice of our justice system, prostitution as an industry, death and the grieving process, disabilities, classism, ageism, homosexuality, substance abuse (including caffeine, alcohol, and prescription drugs), pornography and its effects on people (especially women and children), or the nature of God.

You will need to be careful when you are dealing with a controversial subject. It is easy to assume a righteous stance without exploring the complex nature of the problem. This may come across as judgmentalism, hypocrisy, and closed-mindedness. It's actually okay to say that there is not a good answer to a particular question or that you don't know the answer, but that your faith tells you that God will guide you in time to a place of peace or to a place of action.

People need to struggle with finding answers for themselves, no matter how frustrating it may be for them. Of course, this doesn't mean that you just drop the ball. If you bring it up, you are responsible for traveling with them as they search for answers. Explore the issues as fully as possible, but leave the rest to God.

There will be times when you are very clear about the right Christian response to a controversial issue. In those situations, offer the prophetic word you feel called to share but do so with respect for those who may differ.

Look at your message critically, asking yourself, "Who might be hurt by this message? Have I really explored the issues or am I just parroting back what I've heard?" For example, my sixteen-year-old daughter has troubles just like any other teenager. Sometimes she hears a common church message: "Just give your troubles to God." Her response? "That's NOT helpful!"

Another question to ask yourself might be whether or not traditional teaching on the subject makes some false assumptions. Perhaps there is an alternative interpretation that needs to be considered. As an example, one of the most controversial subjects in the church is on the issue of homosexuality. Like many people, I grew up thinking homo-

The Alternative Worship Primer

sexuals were weird and abnormal. Until I worked for the AIDS Task Force in my hometown, I never had a need to question that stance. As I met gay person after wonderful gay person, I began to see that except for his or her choice of romantic interest or mate, homosexuals were very much like me. Gradually, I learned that they weren't weird. And as I studied psychology, I also learned they weren't abnormal.

But the church had also taught me that homosexuality was a sin. This was rooted in the Bible, of course. I didn't like thinking of my new friends as sinners, so I began to look in earnest at the passages most often used to condemn homosexuals. What I found was quite enlightening. I found that the Old Testament passages either really had nothing to do with homosexuality, or did not consider it any worse of a sin than wearing a garment made of two different fabrics! Jesus had nothing at all to say about homosexuality. Paul's passages on homosexual behavior need to be examined in their historical context. Gradually, I was able to let go of my blinders and see what "the issue" was really about. It's about people, not an act. It's about love, not necessarily sex. And it's about inclusion, not exclusion. Because I allowed myself to struggle, I came to a new understanding. I also recognize that your position on the issue may be different.

For some controversial topics, you may want to offer some additional help to those who may be deeply affected by your treatment of the issue. This may come in the form of a handout which tells people who to contact for help or further information. It may be an offer to speak further with members of the congregation at a different time. It may be the assurance that there are others who are experiencing the same thing (with information on how to get in touch with those people if appropriate).

As you can see from this initial treatment of alternative worship, there are no easy definitions or formulas to follow. It is creative and inspired. If you want to do alternative worship right, you need to be as radical as Jesus was for his day. Be like a prophet: not afraid of being different!

Chapter Three: Why do people want alternative worship?

This question has already been answered, in part, by the previous chapters; but it is a good question to answer in as complete a manner as possible. As the name suggests, alternative worship offers something other than traditional worship. Traditional worship turns some people off, for various reasons. They may not like the pace of the service, the music used, the formality, the length, or even the level of participation expected. For others, they may have experienced something negative in a traditional church setting which, perhaps subconsciously, transfers to every traditional church worship service. Yet many of these same people want a way to learn and grow spiritually in community . . . in other words, in a church setting.

Reasons are many and varied as to why people are interested in a worship service which is not traditional. Let's consider a woman who has not attended church since high school when her parents forced her to go. She was sexually or otherwise abused by her father as a young girl. When she went to church during the long years of her childhood she heard no mention of the type of abuse she was experiencing. Further, she was preached at to love and honor the Father, of whom her earthly father was supposed to be an example. She heard the minister and Sunday School teachers echoing Paul's views that women should be submissive to their husbands and, by extension, women should be submissive to men and girls submissive to boys. She heard the fire and brimstone message that told her she was loathsome and full of sin (which she already believed more than most of us can ever imagine!). She also got the message, either subtly or blatantly, that victims (such as herself, whether she could name it or not) deserve what they get. The church, unfortunately, did not help her. She stopped going to church as soon as she moved out of her parents' house.

Twenty years have now gone by. She believes that God exists and has never stopped searching for the God of which Jesus spoke. She sees that her neighborhood church is offering an alternative worship experience. It sounds interesting and she decides to attend. Imagine how she will feel if the experiences of

The Alternative Worship Primer

her childhood in church are repeated; if she hears a message in any form that women should submit to men because men are spiritually superior; if she is preached at for another twenty minutes about sin and guilt.

Now imagine, on the other hand, that she attends an alternative worship service which is truly alternative. God is referred to as Mother as well as Father. Although it is not the first service she attends, one service is dedicated to opening up discussion on child abuse and its effects on victims, with additional information handed out as to where to find help. She hears Jesus' message of God's love for her no matter what she has or has not done and no matter what she will or will not do about it. She may see in a drama Jesus' challenge to the authorities of today concerning power and discrimination. She also feels the message that God is within everyone, including her.

Wow! What a difference! Perhaps my theology is showing. That's okay. The point is that you need to consider where your theology shows, and what its effect is on people who might be attracted to your church. If you are uncomfortable with some of the ideas presented, then perhaps the type of service you might want to offer would better be labeled a "praise service," rather than alternative. In this type of service you might contemporize the music, add in some performing arts, but stick with the traditional messages that fit your theology. That doesn't mean that some of the ideas presented here won't help you. There's a lot more to it than just changing a message.

Some people are tired of traditional worship experiences. They are tired of sermons, tired of the rigid order of the service, tired of the hymns, tired of the hypocrisy which is sometimes present in traditional teachings, and tired of a narrowly defined God. They are searching for a creative God who respects diversity and opposes injustice in its many forms. They are searching for a place where they can worship in a way that has meaning to them personally. They are searching, perhaps, for a creative outlet themselves.

The Basics

Chapter Four: Who wants alternative worship?

Many church leaders carry the stereotype that those who want alternative worship are only the young people (35 years and under), but this is not necessarily true. Many young people enjoy traditional worship and many older people enjoy alternative worship. As a general rule, the more raucous the music and the more "artsy" the message media, the fewer people of grandparenting age or older will enjoy it and the more people of parenting age and younger will enjoy it. It's a fine line, and you won't know, specifically, who enjoys what, until you do your homework. (See Part II)

Some studies have been done to try to identify generational trends and their relationships to worship. Charles Arn describes three main categories of adults in his excellent and thorough book, *How to Start a New Service:* Seniors (those born before 1946), Baby Boomers (born 1946-1964), and Baby Busters (born 1965-1978). Each of these groups of people have a fairly unique identity and sense of the world. In addition, they also tend to prefer certain aspects and types of worship. Keep in mind that what follows are sociological studies which report general trends. Of course there will be individual differences within each group. But this information may help if you know the general make-up of the audience you are targeting for your alternative service.

Seniors generally like worship services that are slower moving and predictable. They prefer softer lighting and traditional hymns and songs. They want to be able to hear what's going on in the service, but they don't want the sound to blast or boom. They're willing to sit through a service which lasts an hour or longer, but they don't want a high level of participation. They also expect the service to be rather formal. For many seniors, the traditional is sacred and anything which varies from their view of this may be seen as profane . . . or at least unspiritual.

Baby Boomers, on the other hand, like a faster paced service, brighter lighting, and more contemporary, faster moving music. They want fairly loud sound, but they also don't want to be blasted away. Their attention spans are shorter, so they may get fidgety when services reach an hour in length. Interestingly, those Baby Boomers who grew up in the church prefer a fairly high level of participation in the service, while those who did not grow up in the church prefer not to participate. As a whole, Baby Boomers want a service to be organized, but not formal. They are open to new ideas in worship, enjoy variety, and accept a wider range of what is sacred or spiritual.

Baby Busters want the service to move even faster. They also prefer bright lighting and contemporary, fast paced music. They want the sound so loud they can feel it. Their attention spans are even shorter than Baby Boomers, so an hour long service is nearly out of the question. They prefer to be entertained by the service, rather than being asked to participate. And they want the service to be spontaneous . . . or at least appear to be so. Like Baby Boomers, they enjoy variety in their spiritual experiences and are turned off by ritual and tradition.

All this being said, remember that there will be individuals within each of these age groups that "don't fit the mold." There may be reasons which will never be completely understood by either you or the worshiper! Let's take, for example, a senior man who hates organ music. He has always hated organ music and will go on for the rest of his life hating organ music. Perhaps his mother played the organ at home and it caused him to have problems paying attention to what he was supposed to be doing. Because he didn't pay attention, he always got in trouble with his father. He soon learns to associate organ music with being in trouble.

Now, he comes to church and hears, once again, organ music. He doesn't know why, but he gets a very uncomfortable feeling in his solar plexus. He feels a headache coming on. The organ music stops, and he is able to relax. But wait! Here it comes again. And again. And again! He leaves the church that day knowing that something was wrong. He may not know what, but he does know he'll not be back.

Of course, you may also find that the reverse works just as easily. Consider a Baby Boomer woman who has fond memories of her small, hometown church. For whatever reasons, she has been away from the church for several years and is just now looking for a church which suits her needs. She has very definite expectations for a worship service: meaningful prayers, traditional hymns (hopefully some from her childhood), and a sermon which challenges and encourages.

The Basics

Your traditional service would meet her needs exactly, but for some reason, she has shown up at your alternative service instead. She will sit through your service, wondering what has happened that the beautiful church organ doesn't work, sorry that the church choir can only muster four people, and upset that the pastor didn't have time to write a sermon. She probably won't say anything. She'll just slip out quietly after the service and never return.

Although the latter example may seem to carry the message that alternative services are counterproductive, taken together with the previous example, the message is clear. DO YOUR HOMEWORK! Learn as much as you can about your potential target audience. (See Part II) You won't know who wants what until you do your homework.

So what types of people can you expect to attract to an alternative worship service? Beyond the discussion of generational groups above, which points to many Baby Boomers and most Baby Busters, most youth will generally appreciate an alternative service, especially if more contemporary music is used. Parents with younger children may also appreciate alternative worship, even if only because it holds their children's attention better than sermons and long prayers. Creative people (i.e. musicians, artists, writers, etc.) often enjoy alternative worship more than traditional worship. It is understandable, since they are attracted to creativity. You may even be able to entice these types of people to help with the services.

You may also have people in an alternative worship service who were turned off by a bad experience in their childhood church. In Sunday School, a young boy dared to question the meaning of baptism or communion. He was not the type of person to simply be told something and to accept it. He challenged the teacher, and the teacher reacted badly, perhaps humiliating him in front of his peers and getting him in trouble with his parents. He goes on to lead a life of questioning. By the time he is thirty, he is content with his role in life.

He has finally decided to try church again in your alternative worship service. He will be looking for a nontraditional message, one that challenges him and fulfills his need to question. He will be moved by attempts to look at controversial issues without easy answers. He will become one of your greatest assets as you

The Alternative Worship Primer

move forward in your alternative worship endeavor. Since he has felt the oppression of silencing, he may now feel a need for expression. Wouldn't you like to have him on your team of worship planners?

Of course, these are not the only people who will want alternative worship. Churches need to reach out to a variety of people if they want to remain viable. For some, alternative worship is the answer.

Chapter Five: Will some people resist alternative worship?

There is a scientific principle, equilibrium, which basically says that the entire universe resists change. If a particular balance is upset, energy will be expended to return to the balance, to the equilibrium point. So the short answer to this chapter's question is, of course: YES!

There are people within the church who want congregational life to continue the same as it "always" has. I put "always" in quotations because, of course, there is nothing that has "always" been any particular way. These people like the comfort of knowing that there will always be greetings and announcements, followed by an introit, a prayer, a litany, a confession, an anthem, the offering, Scripture reading, sermon, prayer of forgiveness, another hymn, and the benediction. They may even find comfort in hearing the same messages (in slightly varied words) over and over again. They find the rituals of worship comfortable and are upset by change.

Change is stressful, whether we are talking about learning a new skill, altering some type of interpersonal relationship, moving to a new location, or altering the way we worship. Sometimes there is an element of fear involved with this stress: fear of not being able to do something right (failure), fear that resources (physical, emotional, mental, spiritual) will be depleted, and fear associated with the loss of some sense of control. In respect to worship, there may be additional fears which involve a perceived loss: loss of unity of the congregation, loss of sheer numbers of people for the traditional service, and loss of the pastor's attention. All of these fears are valid and should be treated as such. The onus is on the pastor and other church leaders to explore these fears with those who may resist an alternative service. Hopefully, in the process, some fears may be put to rest or at least tamed to a manageable level.

Additionally, there are people who simply lack understanding. Some are of the belief that alternative worship is innately inferior to traditional worship. Remember that the reason they believe this is because of the sanctity they place on traditional worship. You cannot dismiss these sentiments either. When one church was beginning to offer alternative worship along with the traditional service, a woman commented to several others that "it's obvious that those people [who want alternative worship] are just spiritually immature." A handful of people agreed with her . . . or at least chose not to disagree with her. Clearly, education is in order and we will discuss suggested ways to minimize opposition in Chapter 11.

One of the fears of loss mentioned above was the belief that a separate alternative service will take people away from the traditional service. In many ways this is true. If you decide to offer both types of services at separate times, you probably will have some people attending one and not the other. You may also have some who attend both, and some who will start attending only because of the alternative service. It is highly possible that, in this situation, you will have, in effect, two separate congregations in the same building. This would be true, even if the additional service being offered were another traditional one.

You may need to help people understand that most people cannot maintain significant relationships with more than 60 other people in a church or any other organization. This is true if the church has only 60 members; it is also true if the church has 600 or even 6,000 members. Only very small churches have people connecting at a significant level with everyone else in the congregation. Even if there is only one worship service, there are generally multiple sets of connections and relationships. Large churches, of course, are accustomed to this reality already.

In short, you will have people who resist alternative worship, even if you are lucky enough that they are not vocal about it. Be ready for the opposition and integrate it into your action plan. Communicate your openness to the issues that people raise, and convey your continued love and concern for them.

The Basics

Chapter Six: Why should we consider offering alternative worship?

More and more churches are offering alternative worship. It is no longer particularly new, and you can't count on an alternative service automatically bringing in new people. So why do it?

One reason you should consider offering alternative worship is that, if you don't, there may be some people in your congregation whom you will lose to a church that does offer it. If you are at all concerned about declining membership, you should, at the very least, investigate your options and survey existing members. The results may surprise you. You may find that even among those who attend church regularly, there are many who want something different, at least part of the time. If you don't make an attempt, eventually you may lose them.

Another reason to consider alternative worship is that it may provide a more comfortable place for many new people who come in response to the outreach efforts of the church. Keep in mind that, by itself, adding a new service will probably not attract many new people. Your church still needs to proactively reach out to gain new people, whether for a traditional, alternative, or blended service. According to a report, entitled "Proactive Makes the Difference" from New Life Ministries (based on research by New Life Ministries, in cooperation with Christian Community involving over 1,400 congregations and over 250,000 church members), growing churches proactively reach out to twice as many nonmembers monthly as nongrowing churches. And churches that are growing proactively reach out to three times as many nonmembers on a weekly basis as nongrowing churches! The difference is striking! Chapter 12 discusses proactive outreach more thoroughly.

Because a significant percentage of those who come because of your outreach efforts will not have the same strong attachments to traditional worship, they may feel a more comfortable fit with an alternative or a blended service. These services may feel less foreign–or even obsolete–to them.

Still another reason you may want to offer alternative worship is to reach people at a different time of day or different day of the

The Alternative Worship Primer

week. There may be households for which Sunday morning is the only time to relax, and they are not willing to give it up. They may, however, be willing to attend a service on, say, a Thursday evening, or even Sunday afternoon.

Although an additional service may also be traditional, it may make sense for the additional service to provide an alternative style. Sometimes repackaging a message (from a sermon or lecture format) enables the message to connect with more people, especially those who are Baby Boomers or younger, or those who have not grown up in the church.

At this point, we might differentiate two different groups of people who attend church, regardless of age: believers and seekers. Believers are generally people who already believe in God and attend church in order to worship. Seekers, on the other hand, are generally people who aren't sure about God, but who are searching for meaning in their lives. You will undoubtedly have a mix of both at whatever type of service you offer. Although there are some believers who have not grown up in the church, many of them have and they may be quite comfortable in a traditional worship setting. A very large percentage of seekers, on the other hand, did not grow up in the church and are not comfortable with traditional forms of worship. You will want to be sensitive to both categories of people, both in current members and visitors.

Part II–Do Your Homework!

Chapter Seven: Do we need alternative worship?

If you're reading this book, chances are that you already know you **want** to offer alternative worship. But because you want to make sure your time, energy, and material resources are invested wisely, you also need to ask whether or not you **should** offer alternative worship. There is no easy answer to this question. The answer depends entirely on your particular situation. And the only way you will understand your particular situation is to do your homework!

In general, doing your homework consists of two parts. First, you will need to decide who your target audience is. What particular population are you trying to reach? Once you have decided who your target audience is, you will need to find out more about them. What kinds of spiritual attitudes do they hold? What is important to them? How can we best serve them?

Please don't assume you already know the answers to these questions (unless you have already done extensive research). I know of one church which decided that they wanted to reach young adults with young children in the surrounding neighborhoods by offering an alternative service. They were sure there was a great need. They saw several yards with swing sets and driveways with bicycles. But they didn't do their homework. They just jumped right in, announced the new service to the community, and were disappointed when only one or two new persons tried it out. Their effort failed partly because of their lack of foundation. What they found out a few years later is that 75 percent of their neighborhood was of retirement age and were not interested in alternative worship! Many of the swing sets and bicycles were for their grandchildren!

Contrast this with a church–of the same denomination–in that same city. This church definitely did their homework. They researched and planned for over a year before they finally launched their new service. And the results? A large number of members and visitors attended. Enthusiasm for the service (upon entering as a visitor) was palpable. And I'm told that the church as a whole has embraced the concept and supports the new effort, even though not all members attend. Resistance had obviously been handled well.

The Alternative Worship Primer

There are several tools for researching and I would suggest you use as many of them as possible. Consider written surveys (both within your church and the wider community), informal conversations, feedback groups and other gatherings, and telephone interviews. Don't forget about reading books (like this one!) and magazine articles related to alternative worship, as well as contacting church leaders who already offer alternative worship. As will be discussed in Chapter 10, you should have several different people involved in the research. Not only will this spread out the burden of work, but it will also gain you key supporters in the process.

Surveys

You may want to start your research at the easiest entry point: existing members of your church. Perhaps you've already heard from some members that they are interested in the church offering alternative worship. Now, you'll want to know how the rest of the congregation feels about it! (You'll find additional information about survey development in Chapter 8 and sample surveys in Chapter 21.

Start by announcing at least twice that a worship study committee will be asking the congregation to complete short, written surveys on particular dates. Let people know why this research is important. Let people know that you want input from as many existing members as possible. This lets people know that something is coming, lets them feel a part of the direction of the church, and also helps people become emotionally prepared.

Offer your worship survey to those in attendance on at least two, but preferably three, consecutive weeks. This allows you to reach members (and visitors) who may be absent on a particular day. Make sure, however, that you remind the congregation that each person should fill out only one survey so as not to skew the results! By the third time around, you may want to have ushers bring surveys to those who raise their hands (that they haven't yet completed one) or simply announce that there are surveys in the back of the sanctuary for those who have not yet filled one out. Make sure you have a designated place and time to drop off completed surveys. You may choose to collect surveys during worship. You may opt instead to have "Worship Survey" boxes at several locations in your church.

Do Your Homework!

You may also want to include a worship survey in your church newsletter (if you have one). This helps reach those who don't attend regularly, including "shut-ins" and inactive members. Add it as an insert, rather than having it in the main text of the newsletter, as you will want people to mail it back to the church. Again, a reminder about who should complete the survey (those who have not already done so) should be included. If you want a higher response rate, include a return envelope. While you still won't get a huge response, it will be much higher than if you don't. Remember, you want to make it easy to respond!

Hopefully, you also have a list of inactive members and former members. This is an especially important group to reach. They can tell you a great deal about why they no longer attend or why another church meets their worship needs better than yours did. While this information may be painful, it is often quite enlightening. Mail all inactive members and former members a survey. Let them know that their responses are important to the direction of the church. And by all means, include a return envelope. If you have a business reply envelope already made up (postage paid by addressee), use those. If not, consider the possibility of putting stamps on the return envelopes.

For both newsletter responses and direct mail, you will want a deadline date for mailing in the surveys. Make sure it is clearly stated. And set the date at least a week ahead of when you really plan to begin compiling data. Some will surely come in late!

Survey responses from the congregation will be most open and helpful if people are told not to put their names on the forms. You do want to use reminders from the pulpit and through the newsletter to encourage people to complete the surveys. You want to receive surveys back from at least one-third of your average worship attendance. If you typically have 240 present on Sunday morning, you want at least 80 surveys completed.

If your church offers other types of programs, such as support groups, day care, preschool, athletic groups, musical groups, senior coffee & dessert fellowships, teen gatherings, and after school programs, you may want to offer your surveys to those who attend or are members of each of those as well. Remember that each of these programs is an entry point, even if the group only uses your facility and has nothing else to do with the

The Alternative Worship Primer

church. At least it is familiar to them. Who knows? They may be looking for a spiritual community.

You will also want to survey the people in your neighborhood or geographical area who are not (to your knowledge) connected in any way to your church. If your congregation is very large and draws from a large geographical area, then choose the areas you are most interested in targeting. The surveying can be done in several different ways. You can mail them. (Ask the Post Office or a professional mailing firm for instructions and prices.) You can place them in plastic bags and hang them on front doors. (Do NOT place them in mailboxes–it's a federal crime!) Or you can have a team go door-to-door and ask people to complete the surveys while you wait. While this generally gets you a better response, it is also quite expensive in terms of people's time. Most people can complete a typical survey in two to seven minutes. Since you also need to factor in walking time, people not being home, and refusals, you will probably get less than fifteen surveys completed in an hour per person or team. Also, not everyone is comfortable with performing this type of solicitation. Don't ask an introverted person to go door-to-door! People who are comfortable doing this may actually find some new members for your church in the process.

Once you have gathered survey information, have someone–or a team of several people–summarize the results in a short written report. This report will need to be circulated to the worship study committee, various church leaders, and to the congregation. You may want to publish the results in your church newsletter or add it as an insert in a worship bulletin. You may even want to send a mailing to everyone who participated in the study. This type of follow-up creates a sense of good will toward your church. While not everyone will care, it is generally common courtesy to let the participants of any study know the results (and how those results will be used).

Informal Conversations

Although this may seem like a rather unscientific method for gathering information, informal conversations on particular topics can be quite enlightening. Consider for instance, a man who refused to complete a survey on worship. You probably have no idea why he decided not to do this. It may be that he sees it as a waste of paper, since "nothing ever seems to change

Do Your Homework!

around here." It may be that, because he is happy with worship just the way it is, he thought that the survey wasn't intended for him. It may even be that he is having trouble with his eyesight and is embarrassed to tell anyone. The point is that you don't know. If at fellowship time, however, a person on your worship research team talks to him about worship, it may be possible to find out not only why the man didn't fill out a survey, but what he thinks about worship as well. In fact, someone with good people skills who knows what information he or she wants, will probably be able to get the same amount of information or more from the recalcitrant man than if he had actually completed a survey.

Consider, on the other hand, a woman who did complete a survey. Perhaps the survey only told part of the story and she would like to add more. An informal conversation is a way to get her to start talking. She may like to tell the worship committee that unless things change, she'll be leaving the church. Or she may want to volunteer to be a part of the worship planning committee. Maybe she has questions. Again, she probably wouldn't seek someone out to talk to about this, but if someone sought her out, she might open up!

Informal conversations often provide information which clarifies. While a good survey gives information which is quantifiable, a conversation about the information gives depth and perspective. It adds emotion into the equation. It allows an easy way for people to add more to their short answers. It may lead to places of which the worship research team hadn't even dreamed!

One way for informal conversations to take place is to ask those on the research team to target particular people. Choose people you think will be opposed to worship changes, people you think want such changes, and people without strong feelings on the topic. They can arrange to meet with the targeted persons over coffee, during fellowship time after Sunday school, at choir practice, or at another convenient time. Another way for informal conversations to take place is simply to allow them to happen as they will. Have your research team members keep worship research gathering in mind as they go about doing whatever it is they do. Whether they are talking to someone who is of the general age, socioeconomic status, culture or subculture, and spiritual condition your church is targeting for

The Alternative Worship Primer

alternative worship, or whether they are talking about growing the church in Sunday school class, responses usually come to those who ask.

It is important to make written note of conversations, especially if something especially new or powerful came out of the conversation. When the research team meets to discuss results of all the research gathering, a formal written report from each team member on informal conversations is quite helpful. It doesn't need to be long; but key points need to be addressed, including how strongly people feel about various issues and how willing people may be to participate in something new.

Feedback Groups

Sometimes referred to in the business world as focus groups, inviting people to gather together to provide feedback is extremely helpful. You may choose to invite former members and inactive members to a series of coffee and dessert nights in order to be able to ask them questions. Perhaps you'll want to have a free supper for your surrounding neighborhoods. (Be up front about what you'll be asking of them! Don't hide your motives.) Or perhaps you want to hold "cottage meetings" in the homes of your members with other members in the same geographical area invited. You may also want to invite some people to attend your present worship service, then ask them to stay for a (free) lunch and offer their suggestions to lay leaders (without the minister present).

These feedback groups usually offer just what the name suggests: feedback! You may use them to find out what needs the community has that are not being met, what the church is offering that the community doesn't want, what issues and styles of worship are and are not relevant to those you wish to reach, and whether or not your congregation is ready to rise to whatever challenges may be presented.

A gathering of people is often synergistic. One person's idea sparks another. And another and another. People can feel the energy and enthusiasm for some ideas. That enthusiasm can be contagious! At the very least, it may peak someone's curiosity.

Keep the group to a manageable size. If you have fewer than eight participants, the results may be skewed toward the

Do Your Homework!

attitudes and opinions of one or two vocal people. If you have more than twelve, it is difficult to maintain leadership and promote participant interaction. Aiming for 8-12 people should be your goal.

For your focus groups, you will probably want to offer some type of enticement in order to get people to participate. For many, this will mean food! For people in the community with no connection to your church, it could even mean an offer to pay for their time. For others, it may simply mean offering a chance to gather together for the good of the church. For a few, especially those not connected to the church, you will need to be very persuasive, appealing to their desire to make a difference. Make them feel important by personally inviting them to help you, which can be a more effective motivator than paying for their time. It still wouldn't hurt to offer food!

Choose a site for your feedback meetings away from your church. Remember that some people are intimidated by churches. Try to find something more neutral: someone's home; a restaurant with a quiet, secluded room; a school classroom; or a business office.

Set up the room ahead of time. Assuming you are trying for an informal atmosphere (to put participants at ease) you may choose to arrange chairs in a circle or place people around a table (especially if you are serving a meal or a refreshment that's not easily handled). Set up your refreshment table ahead of time as well. People will probably arrive early. Invite them to have cookies, snacks, or beverages as soon as they arrive, even if you are serving a meal. People are more relaxed if they have something to do with their hands.

Choose a leader or moderator for your feedback meeting. This should be someone on your research planning team, but not the pastor. (Again, people may be intimidated by a pastor.) The leader will be the one in charge of asking questions and directing the conversation. Ideally, this person should be skilled in group work. He or she should also be skilled at keeping within a particular time frame, preferably 45 minutes but no more than an hour.

To actually run the meeting, allow a short time for socializing or getting to know one another. This can be done informally by

The Alternative Worship Primer

allowing people to talk to others on their own. It is usually best, however, to have at least some time for a bit more formal introductions. After this, the leader will share the purpose of the meeting, after which he or she will ask questions to which the participants will respond. It is extremely important that the entire group understands that there are no right or wrong answers. The group leader may want to ask clarifying questions or to ask the group what their thoughts are on an issue raised by a participant. It is the leader's responsibility to see that all opinions and ideas presented are treated with respect by all participants. Questions asked by the group leader may be very similar to those questions on a written survey, although they will tend to be more open-ended and less quantifiable. A sample listing of questions on alternative worship may be found in Chapter 21.

You will also probably want someone recording the answers and interactions of the group. While you may choose to tape record the session (You MUST gain consent for this), it is equally viable to have someone simply observe and write notes. People are usually more comfortable without a tape recorder running. Either way, a summary report should be written after each meeting.

Telephone Interviews

Another way to gather information is through the telephone. Although many people are completely fed up with telemarketers, they often don't mind answering questions strictly for research purposes. There are a few "rules" of etiquette to consider before telephoning anyone:

- DON'T call at dinnertime, before 8:00 a.m., or after 9:00 p.m. Although these may be the best times to catch people at home, they are the worst times for people to answer your questions. People don't like it!

- Always tell the interviewee who you are and why you are conducting the research. The more personal you can make it, the more likely the person is to answer your questions.

- Always ask if this is a good time to call. And listen to their answer! If it is not a good time to call, ask when a

Do Your Homework!

good time would be. Record it. Then call back at that time.

- Ask permission to ask questions. Don't assume anything.

Again, the questions you ask may very well be directly from your written survey. On the phone, some people may be willing to go into more lengthy explanation than on a written survey, and those explanations can give you valuable insights.

Books and Magazine Articles

Another important part of your research will be to read. There are several books written specifically for starting a new service, whether alternative, traditional, or some mix thereof. And ministry magazines sometimes focus on starting new services as well. Go to the library and find books. Go to the Internet and find magazine articles. *Net Results* is a publication for clergy and other church leaders which has excellent information on worship. Here are a few book suggestions to get you started:

Arn, Charles. *How to Start a New Service* (Grand Rapids, MI, Baker Books, 1997).

Byars, Ronald P. *The Future of Protestant Worship* (Louisville, KY, Westminster John Knox Press, 2002).

Clapp, Steve, Julie Seibert Berman, Pat Helman and Cindy Hollenberg Snider. *Reaching the Forgotten* (Fort Wayne, IN, LifeQuest, 1997).

Clapp, Steve and Fred Bernhard. *Worship and Hospitality* (Fort Wayne, IN, LifeQuest, 2003).

Schaller, Lyle. *The Very Large Church* (Nashville, TN, Abingdon Press, 2000).

Webber, Robert. *Planning Blended Worship* (Nashville, TN, Abingdon Press, 1998).

The Alternative Worship Primer

Other Churches

Another part of your research will be to visit other churches. Find churches in your area that have been offering alternative worship for a while. Set up an appointment to talk to the pastor and possibly the key worship planners. They will probably have insights applicable to you, especially if you are in close proximity geographically and if you are targeting similar audiences. They will be able to tell you what specifically worked or didn't work for them. They will also probably have some resources to recommend.

Do Your Homework!

Chapter Eight: What should we include in our worship surveys?

The purpose of a survey (and feedback group or interview) is to glean information which will be helpful to you in your planning process. In general, you will need to find out who wants alternative worship. Are there people in your congregation who want it? If so, how many and who are they? Are they interested enough to commit to it in some way? Are there people in your ministry area who are interested and would attend if you offered an alternative service? How much do they want it? And are there certain times for these people that would be better than others?

In general you'll want to keep your survey short enough that most people can complete it in two to seven minutes. It needs to be long enough, however, to give you the information you want and need. There will also be people who feel uncomfortable with certain questions. Assure them that you would appreciate any information they are willing to offer, that the information will be used solely to determine the direction of the church's ministry, and that all information will be kept confidentially within the planning committee. Also let them know that if there is a question they'd rather not answer, that's okay. Some information is always better than none!

For members of your church, the responses you receive will be most honest and open if they do not put their names on the surveys. You want to get some general information to help you interpret the responses: gender, age range, marital status, number of years in the church, and so forth. People in the community may be more willing to share their names on the surveys because they do not have the same emotional investment in how their responses are viewed by others. If they are interviewed in person or over the telephone, their names are of course going to be known. For people in the church and the community, you may want to have a separate form for people to complete, indicating willingness to help with alternative worship. It may simply be a tear-off at the bottom of the survey.

Demographics will play a large role in determining whether or not to offer alternative worship, and if so, what it will look like. (Remember the discussion from Chapter 4.) As a result, several

The Alternative Worship Primer

questions will need to deal with demographic information. For people in the community, you'll want to find out adults' ages, children's ages, gender, education levels, employment status, and occupations. Some of this information will be useful when considering what other programs might be helpful in conjunction with a possible new service. For example, a ministry to people with low income and low educational levels may want to think about offering G.E.D. classes or free tutoring; perhaps a free after-school activity for children. A ministry area with a high income level, on the other hand, may want to offer a women's Bible study brunch or an auxiliary type of group which puts effort into some kind of altruistic endeavor. Or you may want to offer estate planning workshops.

You'll also want to know about church attendance patterns, so you'll need a couple of questions dealing with church attendance. You'll want to know what types of church services people are interested in attending. You'll have some questions that deal with preferences and some that deal with attitudes. While they are related, they are not the same thing.

You'll also want to know whether people are interested in helping with an alternative service. This is a good indicator of commitment. Because you may send the same survey to people in your neighborhood as members of your church, you'll want to find out how many people REALLY want a new service. Conceivably, you could have several people who consistently call for alternative worship, and no one who is willing to help that happen. This may be a good indication that you ought not try a separate service.

Timing is another area you'll want to investigate. Find out what general times people would like to have a worship service. Timing of the service is crucial especially if you are planning a separate service. Although this is a generalization, you will likely attract a greater number of young adults than older adults. While youth may also be more attracted to this type of service, their parents may not be. When to offer the service becomes a critical question and the demographics of your ministry area will help determine the answer.

While each church is different–and your survey will help with this–you might consider Sunday before or after the traditional service (if you want a separate service). Young adults who have

Do Your Homework!

small children may be up and about very early on Sunday morning and they may be glad for something to do with them. On the other hand, some young adults, especially those without children, are out late on Friday and Saturday nights. A Sunday noon service might allow them to attend without interfering with their social lives. Sometimes weekday evenings work, but often people are tired after a long day's work and don't want to go anywhere in the evenings. On the other hand, some people who attend church regularly on Sundays are looking for a midweek worship experience. Friday or Saturday evenings may work for some churches, but tend not to hold up well in Protestant denominations. In short, you won't know what is best for the most people until you ask.

There are sample surveys in Chapter 21. Please feel free to use them as they are, or you may choose to adapt them to your own special needs.

Chapter Nine: Should we have separate services, blended services, or alternating services?

If you have done your homework as outlined in Chapter 7, you may have a pretty good idea of what to expect by offering alternative worship experiences. The results of your written surveys, informal conversations, feedback groups, and telephone interviews will be especially helpful in the process of evaluating whether to have separate alternative services, whether to blend alternative components into existing services, or whether to alternate between traditional and alternative services. Other factors to consider when trying to make this decision may include your current bank of resources, physical facilities, your church's own priorities, and expected tenure of the pastor(s).

First, look at the results from your homework. Is there a clear indication that alternative worship is desired? Does that desire come from both within and beyond your current membership? Is there a clear preference for a time other than the times currently offered? If the answers to all of these questions is an emphatic "yes," then by all means begin planning for your new alternative worship service. Even if you feel your resources are low, this endeavor may very well replenish them. Most likely, you have people who are very enthusiastic about starting a new service that you can call on to take leadership roles in the planning, promotion, and preparation. And as far as financial resources, consider it an investment in the future of your church.

Most churches, however, will not have a completely clear vision based only on surveys and other research tools. There are a few other factors for church leadership to consider. First, consider what your church's priorities are. According to Charles Arn in *How to Start a New Service*, churches which place a higher priority on community rather than on reaching out to new people should not add a separate service. Adding a second service will create a situation in which there are, in effect, two separate churches sharing the same building and the same pastor. For congregations which treasure community quite highly, this will be seen as counterproductive.

Another influence to consider is the role of tradition. Although there are always varying degrees of how highly treasured tradition is in a congregation, there are some churches

Do Your Homework!

which value it so highly that it becomes a splitting maul. Those churches that identify themselves as fundamental, as doctrinally "correct," or as highly heritage-based will have a very difficult time adding a service which will seem to many of the members as "incorrect," fundamentally flawed, or a compromise on truth. Your previous research will, hopefully, give you a good indication of how highly treasured tradition is in your church.

Additionally, churches should not start a new service if the pastor(s), especially the senior pastor, intends to leave in the next two or three years. Charles Arn draws an analogy between a pastor leaving in the midst of a major change to a general deserting his troops. The initiative will be doomed to failure because full commitment and support of the pastor is crucial to the success of any new service. We will discuss this further in Chapters 11 and 15.

Many smaller churches decide that they are simply not big enough to start a new service. Research suggests otherwise in many cases. If your church building is very small, you may very well be limiting your church's growth by offering only one service. As anyone in business will tell you, it doesn't make sense to have a full staff and physical facilities which are not used to capacity. Why should a church be any different?

Some churches, however, are not filled to anything near capacity in the services that are already offered. Churches with average attendance which is 50 percent or less than seating capacity may actually NEED another service. The main reason is that it is highly unlikely that the current service will attract new members. People are not comfortable attending a service which has many empty seats. A new service can attract new people, and you may also be able to locate a new service in another part of the church facility which has a smaller seating capacity.

Don't add a new service for the single reason of keeping your church from dying. Adding a new service for that reason tends to fixate the congregation on the dying process, and that can make church death come sooner rather than later. People are not going to be attracted to your church if they perceive that avoiding death is the main reason for outreach.

If your church regularly fills (or nearly fills) the sanctuary, you probably need to add another service. There seems to be an

The Alternative Worship Primer

optimal point, somewhere between 70 and 85 percent of capacity, where people feel comfortable. If the sanctuary is too full, your church will probably not grow. Statistically, it has reached its saturation point.

Other churches may decide to offer alternative worship services in place of the traditional service on an occasional or regular basis. You may decide to do this once or twice a month. If you choose this option, you will want to advertise which weeks you will be doing which service. In other words, make sure you let people know that traditional services will be held on, say, the first and third Sundays of each month, and alternative services will be held on the second and fourth Sundays. Perhaps the fifth Sundays (of which there are only a few each year) can be something special, such as a celebration, youth presentations, hymn sing-alongs, or a mixture of traditional and alternative worship within the same service.

This type of rotation works well for some churches. It allows an opportunity to offer alternative worship to people who might not otherwise be attracted to an alternative service without completely discarding that which is traditional and comfortable. For other churches, however, it may cause problems. Some people will only want to participate in one or the other type of services. They may begin picking and choosing which services to attend, based on the announced schedule. You may end up with two separate churches anyway. Perhaps this will be an indication to move on to a totally separate service. Some members may go even further and look for a church which does only traditional services or only alternative services. If you've done your homework thoroughly, you should have a good idea of how many members you might expect to lose over alternating services.

These are real dilemmas for the people involved and for church leaders. Although there are steps that may be taken to minimize these problems (see Chapter 11), I personally favor recognizing that this may happen and living with the consequences. You simply can't please everyone all the time, and if you've done your homework and discovered that the need is there, and you truly feel that God is calling you to offer alternative worship, you ought not ignore it.

Do Your Homework!

Support for blended services has increased significantly over the last ten years. These are services that incorporate both traditional and contemporary or alternative elements. In *Worship and Hospitality*, Fred Bernhard and Steve Clapp report on a survey done in 2002 in which 82% of the clergy responding indicated that it was easier to create blended services today than a decade ago. More and more people have friends and neighbors who are attending churches which use alternative worship, and some very traditional people are becoming interested in the impact alternative worship might have on their own congregation. Many of these persons will be open to the blending of contemporary or alternative elements into existing services.

If you eventually want to have all of a service be blended, then you will want a gradual progression. Start small. Add a children's story using a dramatic storyteller. Do this every Sunday until people are used to it. Once this has happened, replace one traditional hymn with one contemporary song. Again, keep at this until people are used to it. (And vary the contemporary style as well. Contemporary doesn't necessarily mean rock-and-roll.) Consider at least occasionally adding drama, contemporary music, liturgical dance, video segments, Reader's Theater, puppets, clowns, pantomime, and so forth. Sometimes, even turning the sermon into a dialogue between two people can add an element of newness. The key is to do it all gradually. Rebellion is usually minimized when changes take place little by little over a long period of time.

Blended services can be a good first step even if a separate alternative service is your final goal. These blended services may offer a drama in place of the sermon, but mostly traditional music. Or they may have a traditional service with puppets and clowns telling a children's story or offering the Scripture, perhaps some contemporary music and some traditional. The possibilities are nearly infinite. Perhaps you'll start out having a blended service every fifth Sunday. Eventually, you may want to offer blended services half the time. Attitudes will probably change over the course of a year or two, if you've offered quality services. When they do, then it's time to do some more homework. It may be time to offer a completely separate service.

Of course, it may very well be that you will find some mix of alternative and traditional which works quite well for your

The Alternative Worship Primer

members and even attracts new people. Not every church will want to move to a separate alternative service or even a blended service all the time. The key is to keep doing some sort of research into the attitudes of members and the community . . . and then to respond to your findings!

Do Your Homework!

Chapter Ten: Who should be involved in the planning process?

It is extremely important for the pastor(s) to be behind the planning of alternative worship and to share ownership for the success of the service(s). Many people in addition to the pastor must be involved in planning, however, if your alternative worship is to be successful. It is important for at least two reasons. First, it's just too big a job for one or two persons. And assuming your church is similar to others, your pastor already has too much to do. Second, those who feel a sense of ownership for a project will support it to the best of their ability. You certainly want that to happen.

You may want to start by recruiting that handful of people who showed interest when you first started asking about the possibility of alternative worship. You will need people to create surveys, recruit survey takers, plan feedback group gatherings, lead feedback groups, gather information from the various sources, and keep the congregation and decision-making bodies informed; you will also need to promote the concept of alternative worship both within and beyond the congregation before and after a decision is made about what it will look like. And you haven't even begun to plan the actual services yet! My own experience has been that the more people you involve, the better your chances of success.

Once you have recruited an initial few, consider asking some influential people within the church who are not in positions of formal leadership to be on an Alternative Worship Study Committee. Be prepared to answer some of their concerns, especially if you know that some of them are the very people who are resistant. Getting them actively involved early in the process allows them to see firsthand that the need is present in the ministry area and within the church. Don't try to sell them on the idea. Let them come to it gently.

Also include your church's more formal leadership. This is crucial. Those who are in leadership positions probably feel called to it. They may feel like it is important to have all decisions go through the formal leadership process (whatever that may be for your particular church). If you bypass this group, they may very well find ways to sabotage your work, as

The Alternative Worship Primer

much as we would like to think otherwise. It has been known to happen that a board or committee meeting has been called at the same time an alternative worship service is going on. This obviously detracts from the service, taking people away from the service, and also giving the message that it's not the "real" service. Do not allow this to happen!

Look around your church. Are there people who are not actively involved but who attend regularly? You might consider asking them to help in the planning process. You may want to stress that it's an important step for the church, but that the commitment also carries with it a definite termination date. In other words, people who are shy about committing to church activity can feel good about their contributions without feeling like they're giving their lives away.

Again, the more people you involve in the planning process, the better. Having a part in it gives a sense of ownership. It won't be just "the pastor's project" or a renegade group of innovators' project (innovators are often seen as renegades!). With the involvement of a wide variety of people, the alternative worship project will be viewed more as a new ministry possibility than simply a project. As well it should be.

Do Your Homework!

Chapter Eleven: How do we handle opposition to alternative worship?

Unless you have a very unusual congregation, you will have some resistance to alternative worship. Even if you blend services, someone–perhaps many someones–will resist. And at times, that resistance can get quite vocal. There are ways to meet the resistance without alienating those who are voicing their concerns.

As the previous chapter discusses, you need to identify the key leaders in your church who need to be part of the process–or who at least need to be persuaded to withhold their disapproval. This may include both formal leaders (officially elected) and informal leaders (respected opinion shapers). The positions and roles vary from church to church. Involving these key leaders in the process or at least communicating with them along the way will help lower resistance.

Keep in mind that liturgies and rituals are often sacred to those who grew up with them. And change is stressful, even when the change is positive. When opposition is encountered, there are generally very real concerns behind it. Do not ignore this opposition. *Ignoring* anything creates an atmosphere of *ignorance*. (Note the similar words!) It is ultimately counter-productive.

One way to approach opposition is as an opportunity. Depending on the individuals in question, you may want to involve a few of those persons in your study committee. This is an opportunity in two ways. One, it will make them feel like they have a voice in what ultimately happens in the church. And two, it will help them see firsthand that a need is present which ought to be addressed. Hopefully, as the process progresses, their own concerns will be addressed and they will be much less likely to oppose alternative worship.

Keep in mind your objectives as you work with people in the congregation. Think about what you want to accomplish with various people. For people whom you know will actively resist a move to alternative worship, you will want simply to get them to a place where they will tolerate it. Don't "oversell" them. It will

The Alternative Worship Primer

probably backfire. Hopefully, as alternative worship blooms in your church, they will move to acceptance, perhaps even support. But if you try to push them toward this, they will feel like they are being railroaded. They may never get to where you want them to be.

There are probably also some people in your church who have vision for your church's future. They will probably see, with a little help from you, that alternative worship is another path for ministry, just as valid as a traditional worship service. You will want to gain their support early on in the process, especially if they are well respected in the church already. You want these persons to speak to others about what an opportunity alternative worship presents for your church's mission, which undoubtedly includes reaching new souls with whom you will share the love of Christ.

Besides the people who were already enthusiastic (whom you want to have actively involved in the research, planning, promotion, and leadership), we are left with the middle-of-the-road people. These are people who either don't have an opinion one way or the other, or can see both positive and negative possibilities. Your "sales objective" for these people is simply acceptance. Like the active resisters, you will not want to push too hard. Answer their concerns, but don't oversell.

You will want to keep open lines of communication with your congregation on a regular basis. Let them know exactly what is happening in the process and what information you have gleaned from your research. People like to know what is going on. Your congregation may be surprised to find out that a sizable group of people in your ministry area would attend a service where drama, dance, and contemporary music are offered, but wouldn't even consider stepping into a traditional service. With this piece of information, they may begin to see the alternative service as a new ministry endeavor, rather than just something that a few people want to do.

To that end, consider making one of the positions on the study committee a communications position. He or she might be in charge of writing articles for the weekly bulletin or the monthly newsletter. He or she might also be charged with communicating in person during the traditional service(s). This person might take special initiatives to reach out to classes and

Do Your Homework!

groups in the church, letting them know about the plans which are being made. And this person may be a liaison to the church board, reporting on the activities, and findings of the study committee.

Open, nonhostile communication is the key whether concerns are being expressed one person to another or at a large gathering of people, such as a board meeting. You may want to revisit the concerns you are likely to encounter (from Chapter 5) and be prepared for them. I would suggest that you and your ministry team become familiar with the next few pages. Most of what follows assumes a separate alternative service, but some of the same fears and misunderstandings are bound to show up in some form or another even for blended services.

FEARS	ADDRESSING THE FEARS
Failure	Failure is always a possibility, but when fear of failure rules our lives, we cease to move forward. Keep in mind that the church has an opportunity which you may feel called by God to act upon. You'll never know for sure where that calling is leading the church until you respond in the best way you know how. Stress that you just can't focus on possible failure. It would probably be a self-fulfilling prophecy!
Lack of Resources	Understanding that it seems like the staff and perhaps the budget are already stretched pretty thin, what you are doing is creating committee or ministry groups to help alleviate some of the staff's work load with worship. Alternative worship is perfectly suited for lay leadership. Adding alternative worship will hopefully bring some new people into the church. If it's successful enough, you may even be able to hire additional staff!
Loss of Control	Knowing that there are people in nearly every church who wish to exert authority over what happens in the church, you might consider offering this type of person a spot on the planning committee. Impress upon

The Alternative Worship Primer

them that the best decisions are those that are agreed to by a diverse group of people. Depending on the persons involved, you might also add that becoming engaged in the planning process will help them be perceived as leaders.

Loss of Unity — Keeping in mind that unity is often more of a perception than a reality, you may remind people that even Jesus' ministry group did not speak as a single voice. Often, it is a very good thing to hear from people with whom we don't necessarily agree. It challenges us to test our belief systems, which ultimately makes our faith stronger. You need to model this in your own relationships with people who are uncomfortable about change.

Loss of People — These people are probably afraid the traditional service will lose people to a new alternative service. Beyond the discussion in Chapter 5, help these people see a bigger picture. If some people choose to "transfer" to the alternative service, doesn't that show a need which is better met by alternative worship? It is quite possible that the church would lose these transferees completely if alternative worship was not offered. Stress that alternative worship will help reach new people, which will strengthen the congregation.

Loss of the Sacred — As mentioned earlier, some people who grew up in the church, hold tradition close to their hearts. Traditional worship is sacred to them. Especially if you are blending your services, rather than offering both types of services, people will fear the loss of something they hold very dear. In this particular case, part of your job will be to find out which traditional elements are most valued and which elements of worship people will most miss if replaced by alternative elements. The other part of your job is to assure people that although there may not be that particular element–say, a

Do Your Homework!

sermon every week–you are not getting rid of it entirely. Explain, in the case of the sermon, that an alternative medium is being used to accomplish the same purpose. (How often you offer any particular traditional worship element will depend on your research and your worship goals.) Then help them understand that you are trying to meet the needs of a diverse group of people. You may want to explain the results of your research and how your current worship goals relate to what you found out.

Inferior Worship

You will undoubtedly, as mentioned in Chapter 5, have some people who truly believe that alternative worship is innately inferior to traditional worship. Your task in this situation is to educate. You may want to talk about Jesus' ministry. There were no pre-set rituals to speak of, no traditional hymns, no particular order of worship. He didn't even have a church building. He adapted his ministry to the situation in which he found himself. He often taught in parables, knowing that stories can touch people's hearts at a deeper level than lectures. In fact, Jesus' ministry style was probably closer to "alternative" than to "traditional."

Inferior Music

Just as you need to educate those who believe alternative worship is inferior, so too will you need to educate those who believe that contemporary, more upbeat music is inferior to traditional hymns and classical organ music. You will want to suggest that people look past the form of the music and pay attention to the words. Many of Martin Luther's hymns that are honored today were written to fit into tavern tunes! Interest in classical music has been in decline in recent years, and fewer young people are learning to play the organ. One can appreciate the quality of classical music and still recognize that a different approach is needed to reach younger people.

The Alternative Worship Primer

Real Church	You will undoubtedly have people who will see the traditional worship service as the "real" church and believe that people can come to that one, rather than an alternative service. Invite those people to extend invitations to the people they know. Assure them that the traditional service is always open to new people. Then also remind them that (perhaps) new people are not attracted to the traditional service for one reason or another, and that the alternative worship service is intended to meet a need which the traditional service does not meet. What constitutes "real" church is whatever offers a safe place for people to gather together for the purpose of worshiping God. Again, the form matters much less than the spirit.

Although every church will have a different mixture of fears and concerns about alternative worship, many of them will stem from those listed above. I would invite you and your ministry team to delve further into the insights presented here. These are not definitive answers to memorize and spew forth. They are starting points for your own understandings of what you are about. The more you explore them and talk about them, the more prepared you will be for whatever resistance may be raised.

Do Your Homework!

Chapter Twelve: How do we promote an alternative service?

Although most of this chapter refers to those churches which decide to offer a separate alternative service, some of the ideas presented may also be useful to those which opt for alternating services or blended services. What I will offer is a smorgasbord from which you may pick and choose. Just keep in mind that the more promotion you do, the more likely you are to attract new people. And promotion works well, even if you are not changing much in your services. It helps to let people know what you offer. Keep in mind that churches which are growing are proactive in reaching out to the unchurched.

The types of promotion you will want to consider include roughly two types: formal and informal. Those who are blending services may choose to focus mainly on the informal promotion ideas, although if it's not been done recently, formal promotion can also have a positive effect. Those who are alternating services will probably want to do some of both types of promotion, especially because you will want to let people know what you are doing when. And those who are offering an entirely new service should give serious consideration to using as many of these ideas (and more!) as possible.

Being Proactive*

Churches which are growing are proactive! These churches are proactive in:

1. Identifying the needs of their ministry areas. They seek ways to help the community in the name of Christ. They become known for their compassion and concern.

2. Identifying people who are not active in any congregation. The church reaches out to them through programs, service, and invitations to attend church.

3. Teaching members and constituents how to talk about their faith and how to invite others to share in worship and other events.

4. Welcoming new people to the congregation and extending Christ's love.

5. Following up on visitors, always within 48 hours of the visit.

6. Integrating new people into the congregation and using those persons in leadership, based on their interests and talents.

7. Evaluating the worship services, Sunday school, other programs, and physical facilities from the perspective of a visitor and making changes when needed.

8. Identifying entry points into the church in addition to worship and Sunday school. They recognize that children's programs, choirs, youth groups, volunteer service projects, support groups, and many other opportunities are potential entry points to the church for new people.

*From "Proactive Makes the Difference," a New Life Ministries Report by Steve Clapp. Used with permission.

Informal Promotion

As with authors, any service (alternative or traditional) has a best friend: word of mouth. The absolute best promotion comes from talking up the service, recommending it to others, and inviting others to attend with you. Currently active members who are supportive of the service need to share their enthusiasm with other members, coworkers, friends, neighbors and family. Encourage the congregation to actively invite others, perhaps offering transportation if needed.

Informal promotion may also include holding a celebration of some sort. Perhaps you will want to throw a yard party, an ice cream social, a picnic, or a free breakfast or lunch. Place a large, colorful sign in your church's front lawn which invites the community in. The celebration itself should be just what it advertises–a celebration. Consider the following possibilities:

Do Your Homework!

- Games for children (of all ages): scavenger hunt, trivia contest (religious or secular), cake walk or other carnival games, or Bingo (if appropriate in your tradition).

- Fun food: pizza, tacos, barbecued chicken, ice cream and cake, pancakes and sausage, baked potato bar, or a fish fry.

- Entertainment (may be previews to your new service): clowns handing out balloons, pantomime show, puppet show, instrumental band, vocal music (choir, small group, solos), liturgical dance, drama, or a talent show.

- Themes: Alice in Wonderland (tea party?), tropical vacation (midwinter works best!), circus or carnival, earth day, or something else!

- Giveaways: balloons, flowers, peanuts, candy, white elephant door prizes, any donated items of some value, cups or pens with the name of your church, brochures about your church, and coupons for a free worship service!

Be creative! The above lists is certainly not exhaustive. Think of a fun event that would draw people to your church and go for it! Keep in mind that you are inviting people to get to know you. Encourage your members to mingle with visitors. Break down some of those invisible barriers that have kept people from walking through your doors. This is not a time to do heavy evangelism, although you will definitely want to announce your plans for a new service and talk about it enthusiastically, both from "the floor" and in individual conversations. And certainly invite people to return. Remember the **reason** for your celebration is the launching of a new type of service. Let it be known!

Formal Promotion

In addition to the informal promotion ideas above, you'll also want to prepare materials to get the word out in a more programmed, formal way. This will include informational flyers, press releases, radio/TV/newspaper advertising, and so forth.

The Alternative Worship Primer

One of the first things to do, especially if you are planning a celebration but also to simply announce your new service, is to create a press release which you will then send to all of the local radio stations, television stations, and newspapers. Most media outlets reserve space for such announcements from nonprofit organizations. (Make sure you contact each station or newspaper to find out exactly to whom and where to send your press release, as well as how far in advance it needs to arrive.) In your press release, which runs from one paragraph to two pages (double-spaced), you will need to include a contact name (so they can contact you if they have questions), and the who, what, where, when, and possibly why. A sample press release may be found in Chapter 21. You may also want to obtain the Christian Community and New Life Ministries resource: *Public Relations Kit* (1-800-774-3360).

Sometimes the event may be newsworthy enough to deserve an interview which results in a full article. If you believe this is a possibility, your press release should be between one and two pages, and you should include a cover letter which ASKS for that. Then you will need to follow up on the mailing of the press release by telephone or e-mail. If you have any hope of this actually happening, **YOU MUST FOLLOW UP WITHIN A WEEK OF SENDING THE PRESS RELEASE.** Don't expect them to contact you. They might, but it is highly unlikely. Call three to five days after sending the press release. Ask if they remember receiving it. Ask if there is any additional information they need. Then mention that a particular person is available for an interview and that you would really like to see a full article, if possible. Be polite, but enthusiastic; be assertive, but not a pest. And be prepared for either a yes or a no.

Additionally, you may want to create a brochure or flier to announce either an event or the launching of your new service—or perhaps both! Make sure you use the three "i's" of marketing: *informative, interesting,* and *inviting.*

You may even want it to look more like an invitation than a flyer or brochure, especially if you are inviting the community to a celebration. If this is the case, enlist a group of people to come together to write out the invitations by hand. In about two hours, you can get at least 200 invitations written by only five people. A handwritten invitation is much more likely to be taken seriously than a photocopied one.

Do Your Homework!

If you have someone who is skilled at desktop publishing, ask them to do a brochure layout for you. If not, you might check at the local high school or at some print shops. They may do it for a fee. Otherwise, enlist someone in your congregation who at the least has an eye for graphic arts. Remember, you're trying to get people interested.

Depending on your budget, you may want to invest in a two- or four-color brochure. Some organizations have four-color laser printers which do an excellent job on small quantities of brochures. Get the most out of your investment by having a professional (or near professional) do the layout. It will be worth it. This is a "sales" tool and what you are offering is something that you feel is of great value to the community.

Now you'll need to distribute your flyer, brochure, or invitation. If possible, recruit some volunteers (your youth group perhaps) to distribute them in person. If they like to meet people, encourage them to ring doorbells and hand them out person to person, rather than leaving them in door handles. If not, there is nothing wrong with leaving them in door handles. (Put them in plastic bags if there is a chance of bad weather!) As I cautioned in Chapter 7, do not place them in mailboxes.

If it is not possible to distribute in person, you can always–for a fee of course–choose to have them delivered by the postal service. Contact them for details. Another option may be to insert your flyers or brochures into neighborhood association newsletters. You will need to contact the association leaders to get information on how to accomplish this. Similarly, your local newspaper may allow you to insert your flyers or brochures into newspaper deliveries. There will probably be a fee involved for this, but check with them to find out what the possibilities are.

Also consider posting flyers in local schools, stores, and libraries. (Get their permission first!) Sometimes posters and flyers can be posted at parks or on telephone poles at busy intersections. Phone calls to city/town maintenance departments should give you an indication of whether or not this is acceptable, and how you should go about doing it. Keep in mind that anything posted outside will need to be durable enough to withstand inclement weather. And it will need to be big enough that people can read it if they will see it from a moving vehicle.

Although some churches will balk at the idea, you may want

The Alternative Worship Primer

to consider paid advertising. Think about who your target audience is. Generally speaking, do they read a particular newspaper? Listen to a particular radio station? Because it would be prohibitively expensive to advertise in all of the local venues, you will want to pick and choose. For those who do choose to advertise, make sure your advertisement uses the three "i's" mentioned above. It should answer the question: Why should we (the community) care?

Keep in mind that people will not know about your new service unless you tell them about it. And they won't care, even after they have heard about it, unless they feel it is useful or beneficial to them. Your job, then, is to let them know about it in a way which conveys your enthusiasm to the extent that visitors (and members) want to join in. To accomplish this, you'll need your marketing hat and your creativity hat.

Do Your Homework!

Chapter Thirteen: What other resources will we need?

The main resource which generally comes to mind when talking about adding anything to the church program, whether it is a new service or a new small group, is money. Although this is an important resource to consider, don't be overly focused on money. There are ways to pay for your new service if you are creative about it.

Especially if you are opting to add a separate service to your existing schedule, there will be additional expenses. You will need to consider honoraria for performers, purchase of music, possible expenses for visual aids, and definite expenses for promoting your new service. In addition, depending on your research results, you may need to offer additional ministries. Will people require child care? Will they want children to attend a type of church school? Is the timing such that you ought to offer refreshments? Will more people be likely to come if refreshments or a small meal is offered?

If you are simply integrating alternative worship into existing traditional worship, your expenses will not be as great, since presumably many items are already covered in your church budget. You may need, however, to generate some extra funding for additional resources and publicity. You may want to create a line item in your annual budget specifically for the alternative service. Until that time, you will want to request permission to use money budgeted for the traditional service.

Depending on your church, you may want to ask a few people who are interested in alternative worship and who have the financial resources to make a donation for the purpose of getting the service off the ground. Or perhaps you will want to take a special offering on a particular Sunday for the alternative service. If you do this, you may want to invite a person from your planning committee to talk about it, and you may want to add an alternative component to the service in order to show the congregation a glimpse of what it will be like.

Once you get the service going, hopefully it will be self-supporting. Money received from those attending the alternative

The Alternative Worship Primer

service might be reserved for supporting the alternative service. At the very least, a line item can be justified in next year's budget, especially if you have several people attending the alternative service who give money to the church.

Besides money, you will also need two other major resources: commitment and people. Without both, your service will fall flat. It is absolutely essential that you gain the commitment of church leaders, including the pastor, the church governing body, and those charged with planning and carrying out the services. Without these, even the best services are doomed to failure.

Remember the example of the meeting called during the alternative worship service? If the church board chair had been supportive of alternative worship, it never would have happened. And if the pastor had refused to be party to such sabotage, it would have sent a message to that church board. Is there a possibility of an influential member talking the service down? If you have involved these key people in the initial stages of research and planning, you have already helped to create a sense of ownership and, therefore, support.

In addition, you will need commitment from those whom you want to plan and carry out the alternative worship services. Too often, a handful of committed individuals bears the entire burden and burnout quickly occurs. To avoid this, you will want to include as many people as possible in the various tasks.

It takes a lot of people to offer alternative worship, especially if you are offering a separate service. Consider finding different people for all of the following tasks:

- Providing music (several - use on a rotating basis)
- Providing drama, storytelling, Reader's Theater, pantomime, clowns, and puppets.
- Helping with readings
- Providing dance or other movement
- Planning and preparing visuals, such as banners, altars, photo displays, etc.
- Working with the sound system
- Providing child care
- Greeting/welcoming/ushering
- Counting and depositing offerings
- Publicity

Do Your Homework!

- Planning services (with the possibility of a different leader each week)
- Follow-up with visitors
- Food preparation/serving

The more people you involve, the greater the probability of success, assuming you have a team of people to coordinate the various tasks. People who have been asked to help in the service will not only attend themselves, but will probably also invite friends and family to come. If you have a separate alternative service, you will want 20-50 people involved, depending on the size of your current church and the depth of your endeavor.

The above list gives you an idea of what tasks need to be covered. It is not exhaustive, so you may very well think of others. And depending on what type of service you envision, you may not need people to do every task on this list. Furthermore, if you are substituting alternative services for traditional services, some of these tasks will already be covered, assuming those people are willing. (But don't assume. Ask!)

You will note in the list that I suggest using more than one person to plan and coordinate the services. This has four main benefits:

1. It provides automatic variety in the types of services offered since individuals vary as to preferences for music, message, media used, and so forth.

2. It provides variety in leadership of the service so that not only can the congregation hear from different people, but it may also offer a creative outlet for people who don't want to preach but feel called to express themselves in a spiritual setting.

3. It spreads out the burden of planning and organizing.

4. It offers a road map for thematic focus.

If your church is large enough, you will probably want to have separate committees for planning and for performing, but keep in mind that some people who want to plan a service, will also want to lead it. One church has a planning committee of six. Their responsibilities are divided up as follows:

The Alternative Worship Primer

- One person plans message themes and type of presentation
- One person finds appropriate music and coordinates musicians
- Two persons coordinate dramatic or other creative elements
- One person oversees the technical aspects (sound, video, etc.)
- One person helps lead worship, coordinate efforts of the committee, and recruit the volunteers for various tasks as needed

Another good idea is to have a group of people who are willing to provide music on a regular basis. Depending on the size of your church, you may want to have an entire choir and band for contemporary music, or you may only want a soprano, alto, tenor and bass, along with an accompanist. With this arrangement, many permutations are possible. For example, one week you might have a soprano solo. Another week you may have an alto/tenor duet. Still another week you might have a quartet, and so on.

In the same way, you might want to have a dramatic committee made up of various people willing to do dramas, storytelling, or some other type of dramatic presentation. Whoever is planning the service, well in advance, would then contact this committee and the committee would decide who should do what. Again, this group of people needs to be committed, but the work needn't be terribly burdensome.

Ideally, your own church members can cover all of the tasks, but it may at times be necessary to invite guests to perform. For example, you may want a liturgical dancer and no one in your church has ever done it. Don't be afraid to ask around. Talented people and groups are always looking for places to perform. Contact larger churches which already provide alternative worship.

Only you and your alternative ministry team will know for sure what challenges you face regarding the resources of money, commitment, and people. Hopefully by now, you're ready to meet those challenges with some creativity . . . and a lot of planning!

PART III–TEST TIME!

Chapter Fourteen: How can we integrate more alternative experiences into our existing worship service(s)?

Many churches, whether because of limited resources or other reasons, may opt to integrate alternative experiences into existing worship services rather than creating, promoting, and sustaining a separate alternative worship service. This is a valid option. If this is the option your church has chosen, go gently! Remember that you will have people who don't like the idea of changing anything which they hold sacred. Remain sensitive to those people who want to retain the traditional format.

One way to ease the transition is to start introducing alternative components into the existing service occasionally. You may want to aim for one new alternative component, such as liturgical drama or dance, once a month for several months in a row. Depending on how it is received, you may move to twice a month either earlier or later than originally planned. You will need to be attentive to informal feedback from those in attendance.

Once your congregation is comfortable and familiar with alternative elements every so often, add more components into the service when the calendar calls for alternatives. Try substituting drama or video for the sermon; substituting contemporary music for traditional; adding in clowns, pantomimes, or puppets. Reread Chapters 1 and 2 for additional ideas. Before long, you may have a regular schedule of traditional and alternative services with which your congregation is familiar and comfortable. Whether the alternative service comes once a month or every other week, you'll have added helpful options to the worship experience.

You may decide that you do not want to work toward alternating between traditional and alternative worship. You may opt to simply offer alternative components, blended into every service. This is another valid option. Again, I would suggest that you work toward this slowly in order to minimize resistance. Don't start out by changing the sermon. Add something extra at first, like clowning or a puppet skit. Try out

The Alternative Worship Primer

various styles of contemporary music, in addition to the more traditional music. Invite a dancer to interpret your choir's anthem. Use a video clip to add depth to a sermon. Substitute for the sermon only after you have successfully used other alternative components in your existing service.

These are perhaps the easiest ways to integrate some alternative components into an existing traditional service. Remember the ideas in Chapter 2 and add your own. Use your imagination. Make the service come alive.

> *You may find it beneficial to involve Sunday school classes and other groups in your church in a study of the relationship between worship and hospitality. When people begin to be concerned about meeting the needs of others in worship, they become less fixated on having every element in worship conform to their own tastes.* **Worship and Hospitality** *by Steve Clapp and Fred Bernhard is an excellent book for that purpose.*

Test Time!

Chapter Fifteen: How involved should the minister be in the service?

It is very important for the pastor to be present even if he or she hasn't planned much of the service. In multiple staff churches, a staff member other than the senior pastor may be the person normally involved in the alternative service, but you still need the senior pastor's presence at least part of the time. People who attend an alternative service will pick up subtle messages about the importance of the service based on who is and is not present. If the pastor is not present, that tells people the service is secondary or not as important as the traditional service.

It is very helpful to have the pastor present to greet and welcome those who attend the alternative worship service. This sends a powerful message: "You are important enough for me to be here to welcome you." Visitors especially are more likely to return to a church where they have been greeted warmly by a minister of the church.

How much a role the pastor has in the service beyond welcoming people depends on the specifics of your situation. If it is a blended service, obviously the pastor will be involved in almost all of it–with help on tasks like drama from others. If it is a separate alternative service, leadership of many components may come from other persons with the pastor participating in ways that seem most comfortable.

When congregations have a separate alternative service, there is a tendency for the pastor to give the same sermon at that service as was given at the traditional service(s). The visibility of the pastor in that way has positive impact. Having a traditional sermon each week, however, diminishes some of the benefit of having an alternative service. Drama and video should be used at least part of the time, either as substitutes for the sermon or as complements to the sermon.

The Alternative Worship Primer

Chapter Sixteen: Where can we find music and musicians appropriate for an alternative worship service?

Music will be an important component for most alternative worship services. Both the message and style of music will be scrutinized and judged.

You may want to have an alternative music director, whose function is to suggest appropriate music for various themes of worship. This person may be on your Alternative Worship Planning Committee. He or she could then assign specific pieces to the various musicians who have volunteered to provide music for the services. (Recall the various tasks in Chapter 13.) Of course, you may decide that this will not work for your church, perhaps because you have no one interested in this task. You have another valuable resource: your congregation itself, your youth in particular.

You may want to ask your youth to listen for contemporary songs that would fit various alternative worship themes, whether or not you employ an alternative worship music director. Often, there will be a number of youth and young adults who listen to contemporary Christian radio. They can be an invaluable resource. Recruit them for your Planning Committee if possible.

Also, don't forget that many popular secular songs are appropriate for alternative worship. Secular radio stations, especially soft rock stations, often play songs that can be used in appropriate ways. Any songs that deal with real love (as opposed to a hormone rush), grief over injustice, death of a loved one, the strength of the human soul, a person's good character, discrimination, or one that contains a eulogy for a respected person might be used for alternative worship. Again, it is most helpful to have at least one person who is constantly listening for songs to use in worship. Still, it doesn't hurt for many people on the Planning Committee to keep an ear open!

Many denominations are offering more alternative music suggestions or integrating such music into new editions of hymnals. These are excellent sources because the theology will

Test Time!

be consistent with your denominational heritage. Chapter 18 offers additional suggestions.

As mentioned earlier, high school choirs and bands are often looking for outlets to perform. However, if you have particular songs you would like a choir to sing or a band to perform, you may have better luck asking an elementary school or middle school choir or band. They are not as likely to be rigid about their repertoire since they don't participate in music contests as much as high school choirs and bands.

Even if the school choirs or bands can't accommodate you, an announcement by a director in those classes may bring results. If you ask for a quartet that would be willing to sing for a small honorarium, you may get enough volunteers that you'll need an audition!

Don't stop at the schools! Perhaps there are other youth organizations to whom you may make a request. Is there a children's choir in your area? Are there women's or men's musical groups? Is there a coffeehouse in your area which features aspiring musicians?

Check with other churches in your area. Whom do they use? Are they available to your church? Would they be interested in an occasional "swap?" And don't forget to put the offer out in your own church. Even small churches usually have young (or even older) people who want to perform contemporary music. Don't overlook your own!

Chapter Seventeen: How do we define success with alternative worship?

In our culture we often define success in numerical terms. Rapid, continual growth is key. Few other factors are taken into account. Often, the various entities which experience rapid growth have very little foundation and they rely on more and more gimmicks to continue. In worship, we need to gain a larger perspective.

First, do not make a judgment regarding the success of your new service any earlier than one year from its original kick-off date and perhaps even two years. Remember that anything new takes time to get rolling. Mistakes are inevitable in any new endeavor. Give yourself room for those mistakes.

Second, attendance should not be the only indicator of how well a service is going. If attendance is still dismally low after a year, you may want to do some further work to discern where the problems lie and whether or not there is enough interest from these involved to actually work to correct those problems. Sometimes, however, attendance can be low for a long period of time while the service itself meets the spiritual needs of those who do come. There are many factors which might contribute to low attendance, especially poor publicity. Attendance is not enough for evaluating a service's "success." It is only one factor.

Consider your original reasons for starting a new type of service. To whom do you want to reach out? Have you reached them? Who felt called to be a part of this ministry? Do they still feel so called? Does the service support itself? Does it need to?

All of the above noted, you will also need to determine whether or not your church can sustain a service if it is not self-supporting. Obviously, you can't keep a ministry going forever if it drains you of your most valuable resources: people, energy and, of course, money.

In order to evaluate effectively, you will want to survey those in attendance. You will want to ask questions about the overall quality of the services, the appropriateness of the service themes, the length of the services, the music, the flow of the service, and

Test Time!

the way the messages were delivered. You will also want to know how meaningful the services are to those who attend. How has it affected their worship experience at your church? How important is this service to them?

Ideally you will already have a worship evaluation team set up ahead of time. This group of people will ultimately make a recommendation for or against continuation of your service to the leadership of the church. Evaluation by this committee should include such items as average attendance, timing of the service, leadership, coordination, variation, music, and messages offered. Evaluation criteria may have been decided upon and made up during the planning stages of your alternative worship project. This is often ideal because the items considered in the evaluation are less likely to be subjective and more likely to be appropriate to the goals of the service.

Start with the assumption that the service is successful if it meets a relatively high percentage of the original goals. You may want to weight them mathematically in accordance with your priorities.

Weighted Goals Example

Suppose your original goals for a new alternative worship service was to have 50 people in attendance each week, to offer a creative outlet for members who feel called to a less formal ministry, and to reach out to both new and returning young adults. Your evaluation team may find that attendance has averaged only 30 people per week, but it has met the other two goals in a powerful way. Perhaps 20 of the 30 people regularly are young adults and half of them are new! Your weighted score may look something like this:

Goal	Priority	Weight	Score	Weighted Score
50 in attendance	1	(50%)	60	30
Creative needs met	2	(30%)	100	30
Reach young adults	3	(20%)	90	<u>18</u>
				<u>78</u>

The Alternative Worship Primer

In the "weighted goals example," our overall score is 78 (on a 100 point scale). Not great, but perhaps not bad enough to warrant canceling the alternative service. It also may point to the fact that perhaps the number of people in attendance isn't really as important as thought originally and you may decide to adjust your priorities.

Only you will know what your priorities are and how much weight to give them. Only you will know if the drain on finances and people is too much to sustain. Only you will know if the service has become enough of a ministry to warrant its continuation regardless of the original goals.

Test Time!

Chapter Eighteen: What other resources are available?

In answer to this question, I could almost say the sky is the limit! Look for books of poetry, drama, and music. Whenever you watch a movie, think of its values for alternative worship. Look for children's stories which can be told in a service. Check into a nearby fine arts collective or organizations for performers. In other words, bring the rest of the world into your church and make it holy!

Following is a list of books, song books, videos, and catalogs which might be helpful to you. This list is not exhaustive by any means, but it may give you a place to start.

Nontraditional Worship Resource Books:

Alternatives for Worship by Cindy Hollenberg Snider and Steve Clapp. 1998 Christian Community. ISBN: 1-893270-00-9. Twenty complete nontraditional services, including all text and suggestions for music.

Creating Quality in Ministry by Steve Clapp and Cindy Hollenberg Snider. 1995 LifeQuest. ISBN: 0-9637206-6-X. Includes a chapter on nontraditional worship considerations as well as general information on quality in worship. Also includes surveys and check lists.

Let All Within Us Praise! by Patricia J. Shelly. 1996 Faith and Life Press. ISBN: 0-87303-208-X. Dramatic Readings and original songs for nontraditional worship. Includes worship planning notes.

Worship and Hospitality by Steve Clapp and Fred Bernhard. 2003 LifeQuest. ISBN 1-893270-16-5. Help in relating hospitality to worship. Includes many suggestions for creativity with sermons and sermon alternatives.

Books of Poetry / Prayer / Readings:

Guerrillas of Grace by Ted Loder. 1984 LuraMedia. ISBN: 0-931055-04-0. Probing prayers in poem form. Don't be

The Alternative Worship Primer

fooled by the 1984 copyright–these prayers are compelling and contemporary.

Heard in Our Land by Dr. Eugene Roop. 1991 FaithQuest. ISBN: 0-87178-351-7. Poetic prayers for every season.

Psalms/Now by Leslie F. Bradt. 1973 Concordia Publishing House. ISBN: 0-570-03230-X. Contemporary versions of the Book of Psalms.

The Black Bible Chronicles: Rappin' with Jesus by P.K. McCary. 1994 African American Family Press. ISBN: 1-56977-005-0. African American version of the four gospels.

The Inclusive New Testament. 1994 Priests for Equality. ISBN: 0-9644279-0-7. A nongendered version of the books of the New Testament.

Possibilities for Video Clips:

28 Days - Addictions & recovery; Responsibility for self; Acceptance
Angels in the Outfield - Need for love; Sacrifice
The Cider House Rules - Humanity beyond rules
Contact - Vastness of creation; God's endless possibilities
Finding Forester - Making a difference in the lives of others; not judging people too quickly
Good Will Hunting - Compassion; Using one's God-given gifts
The Green Mile - Prejudice; Healing power of love
Jacob Have I Loved - Judgmental attitudes and their affect
Miracle at Moreaux - Misunderstandings which lead to prejudice; Helping others
Phenomenon - Value of individuals; Understanding beyond limited perspectives
Pocahontas - Violence against people; Violence against nature
Powder - Prejudice and intolerance; Beauty of humanity
Schindler's List - Take risks for the sake of others
Seasons of the Heart - Grief and healing; Giving versus withholding love
Seabiscuit - Overcoming barriers; striving to be one's best
The Secret Garden - Healing through love
The Shawshank Redemption - Hope; Kindness in oppressive situations

Test Time!

Steel Magnolias - Dealing with loss; strength of character
Titanic - Cycles in life; dreams; courage

Note: Some of these movies have strong language, violence, and sexuality. Choose the clips you will use carefully.

You may also want to examine the suggestions of Craig Brian Larson and Andrew Zahn in their book *Movie-Based Illustrations for Preaching and Teaching* (Zondervan, 2003). That book includes 101 reviews of film clips.

Song Books:

Bring the Feast: Songs from the Re-Imagining Community. 1998 The Pilgrim Press. ISBN: 0-8298-1254-7. Ethnically diverse, gender-inclusive music for contemporary worship.

Cokesbury Chorus Book I. 1996 Abingdon Press. ISBN: 0-687-01888-9. Contemporary and traditional worship songs.

Come Celebrate! 1995 Abingdon Press. ISBN: 0-687-01698-3. Songs for contemporary worship.

Drama Resources (request catalogs):

Contemporary Drama Service, 885 Elkton Drive, Colorado Springs, CO 80907. (719) 594-4422

Willow Creek Resources, P.O. Box 3188, Barrington, Illinois 60011. (800) 470-9812

The Alternative Worship Primer

Chapter Nineteen: What do copyright laws really say?

Copyright laws are intended to protect the owner of the copyright, usually the author, publisher, or producer of a work, from unauthorized free use of a work of art. This includes print works, fine art, music, other sound recordings, and film. Unauthorized copying or use of a work of art in effect is stealing from the owner of the copyright.

The laws governing copyrights are quite specific. Unless permission is granted otherwise in writing and ahead of time, you may not photocopy music, poems, prayers, skits, plays, stories, books, and so forth for distribution to your congregation. This is why enough song books and hymnals for the entire congregation must be purchased in order for a church to use them. In the same way, you may not record someone else's music off the radio and use it in a public setting. Copying videos is similarly illegal. And unethical.

There are differences of opinion on how copyright laws apply to the use of materials in worship. Worship services are more educational than entertainment in nature. As a result, some uses should be all right under the educational provisions of the copyright laws. If you want to be completely safe, there are license arrangements you can make as shared at the end of this chapter.

Showing a video clip during a worship service should fall within the intention of the copyright law, which gives permission for face to face teaching activities. Care should be taken, however, to give full credit to the original work. In case of the movies, you should list the title, the year of its release, and the movie company which produced it. Check the copyright listing on the package to determine if the copyright owner is different from the producer and should also be given credit.

Additionally, copyright laws allow the public display of a purchased work of art if the work in and of itself is not the main emphasis and if there has been no fee collected for the viewing of the work. Again, credit must be given where credit is due. So, in the case of using recorded music for a worship service, you may

Test Time!

purchase a cassette or CD and play it for a worship service, assuming that the worship service is free of charge and that you give full credit in some way to the artist/copyright owner. The best way, if you have a bulletin, is to list it there. If not, you should verbally tell the origin of the music played.

Further, a worship service is generally considered a teaching activity rather than entertainment. Because teaching activities have a different purpose than pure entertainment, the copyright laws treat them differently. For example, showing short clips from videos (3 to 8 minutes in length) as suggested in the previous chapter would fall into the category of a teaching activity. Showing an entire movie runs the risk of falling into the entertainment category and may not be allowed.

If you ever run into a situation where you are unsure as to how to apply the copyright laws, it may be best to either consult an attorney, or call the copyright owners (or those who work closely with them). Purchase enough song books for every one, photocopy only with permission in writing, give credit where credit is due, and ask if you don't know. If you do this in good faith, you can be fairly sure you are not cheating an artist out of his or her "paycheck."

These laws are in a state of change, and authorities do not always agree on interpretation. I am sharing the best information available at the time of this printing, but I am not an attorney.

Many churches are obtaining licenses from the Christian Copyright Licensing International organization. Their website can be found at www.ccli.com. This company provides licenses for music, videos, and events.

Part IV–Graduation

Chapter Twenty: So, may we review please?

If you've read this book carefully, you've gotten a lot of information in a fairly short period of time. You may be wondering how to go about putting it all together. What follows is a checklist for a church which is seriously considering adding an alternative worship service to its existing schedule or moving toward more blended services. I have suggested this checklist as a response to what an average size church might experience. You will need to set your own time line for accomplishing all that needs to be done. Just two words of caution: DON'T RUSH!

Permission to photocopy the following checklist is hereby granted to purchasers of this book for use within your own church. Please feel free to modify it to suit your own specific needs as well.

- ☐ Decision made to investigate Alternative Worship.
- ☐ Begin asking questions of church leaders, creative individuals, youth, young adults, etc.
- ☐ Make a list of interested people.
- ☐ Ask some of those on the list to be a part of the Alternative Worship Committee (AWC).
- ☐ Informally let key leaders know what you are doing and why!
- ☐ Set an initial meeting date for the AWC.
- ☐ Hold the initial meeting of the AWC:
  Hand out photocopied material, books, etc.
  Introduce idea of homework. (Surveys, meetings, informal discussions, etc.)
  Assign various tasks: chair or co-chairs, secretary, survey drafting, recruiters
  Set next meeting date.
- ☐ Secretary gives written report to Pastor, AWC members, church leaders.
- ☐ Draft initial surveys (see the next chapter).
- ☐ AWC meeting:
  Strategize about surveying current members, inactive members, former members, and the surrounding community of nonmembers.
  Revise surveys as photocopied or drafted to fit your needs and interests.
  Set target date for survey implementation.
  Assign recruiters specific people to target for various tasks.

The Alternative Worship Primer

- Secretary writes written report for key leaders as well as members (via newsletter, bulletin, announcements)
- Next AWC meeting:
  Final revisions of surveys. Who will make copies?
  Review people recruited to help implement survey process. Make sure your bases are covered!
  Target date: revise or okay?
  Assign tasks for process to begin.
  Introduce ideas about how to handle resistance.
  Begin plans for cottage meetings or discussion groups:
  - Purpose?
  - Who will lead?
  - Format?
  - Dates?
  - Where will they be held?
  - Other resources needed?
- Surveys via bulletins for members and visitors in attendance. Provide instructions.
- Surveys mailed to inactive & former members. Follow-up with phone call or surveys done via telephone.
- Surveys into neighborhood.
- Article and survey in newsletter.
- AWC meeting:
  Initial results of surveys.
  Response rate - need to improve? How?
  Finalize plans for cottage meetings/discussion groups:
  - Meeting place(s)
  - Date(s)
  - Focus
  - Leadership
  - Format
  - Invitations
- Written report to key leaders/board/elders.
- Implement plan for getting more responses.
- Continue with informal discussions.
- Cottage meetings/discussion groups held.
- Written reports from each meeting to Secretary.
- AWC meeting:
  Reports on cottage meetings/discussion groups.
  Assign survey tabulation tasks.
  Discuss problems encountered, including resistance.

Graduation

- Survey tabulation complete.
- Written report to church leaders / Board / Elders.
- Written report to members (via newsletter, bulletin)
- AWC meeting:
  Discuss overall results of surveys, meetings, discussions.
  Draft initial proposal to Board / Elders.
  Assign thank you tasks for those recruited.
  Assign one or two people task of revising proposal.
- Initial proposal revised for presentation to AWC.
- AWC meeting:
  Revised proposal reviewed.
  Final editing of proposal.
  Contact Board/Elders to get on agenda.
- Secretary gets proposal in presentation form.
- Entire AWC present at Board/Elders meeting for presentation of proposal.
- AWC meeting:
  How did it go?
  What was the outcome?
  Further work to be done? How? By whom?
  Now on to planning the service?
  Who might be interested in being on the Alternative Worship Planning Team? (AWPT)
  Check surveys for clues!
  Who will contact these people?
  Who will be liaison(s) to AWPT?
- Formal report to members.
- Recruit people for the AWPT:
  Writers
  Musicians
  Actors
  Dancers
  Technical people
  Creative people
  People who need to express themselves through this ministry.
- Set target date for first Alternative Service–at least three months from now.
- Set first meeting date of the AWPT.
- First AWPT meeting:
  Overview by AWC liaison.
  Formulation of worship themes.
  Assign tasks for at least first two months' services:

The Alternative Worship Primer

        Service writing
        Music coordinator
        Coordinator for performers other than
        music (actors, storytellers, readers,
        dancers, clowns, puppeteers, mimes, etc.)
        Publicity Coordinator
        Coordinator for other tasks (ushers, food
        preparation, child care, etc.)
        Special event for kick-off?
        Liaison acts as Secretary (reporting to AWC,
        Board/Elders, etc.)

- Publicity coordinator writes press releases, bulletin announcements, invitations, flyers, brochures, etc. Distribute to:
      TV
      Radio
      Newspaper
      Community
      Direct mail
      Church
- Coordinators begin contacting interested individuals for various performing teams.
- Writers contact coordinators for needed performers.
- Coordinators contact performing team members for specific requests.
- Other task coordinator lines up people to cover various tasks - including kick-off event.
- Regular meetings set up for AWPT.
- AWC meeting:
  Report from AWPT liaison.
  Begin to decide evaluation strategy:
      How?
      When?
      By whom?

    The above checklist may not be exhaustive. As you go through the process, you may find that your particular situation calls for adding some items to the list, substituting some items for others, or deleting some items altogether. Use it as a guide, but not necessarily a final authority. By the time you reach the end of the checklist, you will be quite familiar with your own process and what needs to be done. You will have graduated and moved on to the real world of Alternative Worship!

Graduation

Chapter Twenty-one: What notes may we take with us?

The following pages present samples of various items you may need to write in the course of your journey with Alternative Worship. Permission to photocopy these materials is granted to purchasers of this book for use within your own church. Please feel free to modify any sample to fit your own particular needs.

Graduation

Survey #1 - Active Members / People in Attendance

1. Are you a (check one):
   __ first-time visitor __ visitor who has attended before
   __ member   __ constituent

2. How would you rate the overall quality of the worship service (check one)?
   __ Excellent __ Good __ Fair __ Poor
3. Is the service (check one):
   __ too long __ too short __ just right
4. How would you rate the music?
   __ Excellent __ Good __ Fair __ Poor

5. Check any of the following variations in worship which you might find meaningful or helpful:
   __ drama or skits, storytelling, Reader's Theater
   __ contemporary music
   __ more variety in musical instruments
   __ more contemporary language
   __ more inclusive language
   __ liturgical dance
   __ puppets, mimes, clowns
   __ shorter services
   __ services without a sermon
   __ more challenging or controversial topics
   __ more congregational participation
   __ short clips of motion pictures
   __ a service on a different day/time
      (please suggest: _____)

6. Would you be interested in attending an alternative worship service which might include some of the items listed above?
   __ yes, regularly __ yes, occasionally __ yes, rarely __ no
7. Would you be willing to help with such a service?
   __ yes, regularly __ yes, occasionally __ yes, rarely __ no

8. __ Male or __ Female
   Age range: __ 65 or older __ 50-64 __ 35-49 __ 19-34
              __ 13-18 __ 12 or under
   Years a member of or connected to this church:
   __ Less than a year __ 1-3 years __ 4-7 years __ 8-15 years
   __ 16-25 years __ 26 years or longer

The Alternative Worship Primer

Survey #2 - Inactive and Former Members

1. Name _____
   Phone #_____ e-mail _____
   Address _____
   _____

2. How long has it been since you have attended our church? _____

3. How long has it been since you have attended any church? _____

4. For what reasons did you stop attending our church? (Check as many as apply.)
   __ People were unfriendly.
   __ My schedule doesn't allow me to go to the service(s) offered.
   __ The service was boring.
   __ The service held no meaning for me spiritually.
   __ I don't feel I need church.
   __ I hate sermons.
   __ My children are out of the house, so I'm done with church.
   __ The overall program of the church did not meet my spiritual needs.
   __ The physical facilities turned me off.
   __ My children didn't like attending.
   __ I don't like church music.
   __ I don't believe in God.
   __ I feel like most Christians are hypocrites.
   __ Other: _____

5. Is there any change in the worship service which would cause you to return? (Check as many as apply.)
   __ Shorter service.
   __ More drama, Reader's Theater, storytelling.
   __ Use of video.
   __ Different day/time. (Suggestion: _____)
   __ More interaction during the service.
   __ More contemporary music.
   __ More inclusive language.
   __ Use of liturgical dance.
   __ Use of puppets, clowns, mimes.
   __ More challenging messages.
   __ More messages which I can apply to daily life.

Graduation

   __ More messages on controversial or tough issues.
   __ No sermons.
   __ Chance to participate actively in planning or leading services.
   __ More celebration of God's love.
   __ Less judgment from members.
   __ Other: _____
6. Would you be interested in attending a new alternative worship service which would be more contemporary in nature?
__ Definitely __ Probably __ Maybe __ Doubtful __ No way
7. Would you be interested in helping to plan such a service?
__ Definitely __ Probably __ Maybe __ Doubtful __ No way

The Alternative Worship Primer

Survey #3 - Nonmember Community

Please complete the following questionnaire as completely and accurately as possible. Thank you in advance for your time.

1. Name _____
    Phone # _____ e-mail _____
    Address _____
    _____

2. Are you a member of a church?
    __ yes   __ no   __ I'm not sure
3. Have you ever been a member of a church?
    __ yes   __ no   __ I'm not sure
4. Are you currently attending any church?
    __ yes, regularly   __ yes, irregularly   __ no

5. If you answered "no" or irregularly to question four, what keeps you from attending church? (Check as many as apply.)
    __ Church people are unfriendly.
    __ My schedule doesn't allow me to go to the service(s) offered.
    __ Church services are boring.
    __ Church services hold no meaning for me spiritually.
    __ I don't feel I need church.
    __ I hate sermons.
    __ My children are out of the house, so I'm done with church.
    __ The overall program of the church doesn't meet my spiritual needs.
    __ My children don't like attending.
    __ I don't like church music.
    __ I don't believe in God.
    __ I feel like most Christians are hypocrites.
    __ I'm of another religion. (Which? _____)
    __ Other: _____

6. Which of the following, if offered at our church, would make you more likely to attend? (Check as many as apply.)
    __ Service lasting no longer than 45 minutes
    __ Drama, Reader's Theater, storytelling
    __ Use of video
    __ Interaction during the service
    __ Contemporary music
    __ Inclusive language

Graduation

- __ Use of liturgical dance
- __ Use of puppets, clowns, mimes
- __ Challenging messages
- __ Messages which I can apply to daily life
- __ Messages on controversial or tough issues.
- __ No sermons
- __ Chance to participate actively in planning or leading services
- __ Celebration of God's love
- __ No judgment from members
- __ Other: _____

7. If you checked any item in question six, is there a particular day and time which would suit you best? Please list your top three preferences:
   day: _____ time: _____
   day: _____ time: _____
   day: _____ time: _____

8. If we offered an alternative, contemporary service, how likely would it be that you attend at least once a month?
   __Definitely __Probably __Possibly __ Probably not __No way

Thanks for completing our survey.
Your input is very important to us.
Please return it in the enclosed postage paid envelope.

The Alternative Worship Primer

Sample Press Release

For immediate release . . . Contact: Alan Alt (101) 555-8822

Chosen Church Buries Stereotypes!

So you thought church was boring? Sleepy music and lectures disguised as sermons? Think again. Chosen Church, located at 111 Sanctuary Drive, is ready to bury those stereotypes!

Chosen Church is starting a new, alternative worship service on Thursday evenings from 6:30 to 7:15 p.m. with a light supper being served – free of charge! – beginning at 5:30 p.m. The supper and the service begin next Thursday, September 18th. Spokesperson Alan Alt says the new service will be more contemporary. According to Alt, "We'll use lots of drama, contemporary music, video, clowns, puppets, liturgical dance, and other fun stuff." Alt further assures us that there will be no sermons! A church service without sermons? Are you kidding?

Apparently, they're not. For more information, contact Alan at 555-8822, or visit their website: www.chosenchurch.com. Or stop by and check them out! Everyone is welcome!

Graduation

Sample Invitation
Best if handwritten!

The Celebration
What: *A new, contemporary worship service*
When: *Thursday, September 18, 6:30 p.m.*
Where: *Community Church, 111 Sanctuary Drive*

The Invitation
*Join us for a FREE taco bar at 5:30 p.m., followed by
a short celebration of God's love, and ending with
FREE ice cream at 7:15 p.m.
We hope you'll join us for a fun-filled, joyous evening!*

*Child care available for those attending.
Call the church ahead, please (555-8822).*

RSVP is appreciated, but not necessary. 555-8822

The Alternative Worship Primer

Chapter Twenty-two: Any final hints?

You've got the basic information. You've done your homework. You may be in the midst of planning for your first alternative worship service. The best advice I can give you at this point is to relax and enjoy the journey. You will undoubtedly make mistakes along the way. These are rarely fatal, at least if you are paying attention!

A few minor details about alternative worship may be helpful. (1) I would suggest offering music 10-15 minutes before the service begins. This "gathering music" may be performed live or prerecorded. It will set the mood of the service. . . so choose carefully! (2) One church I visited made a special announcement about the offering with was directed to visitors. It went something like this:

We collect an offering each week to fund the ongoing ministries of our church. If you are a visitor, please consider this service our gift to you. Please do not feel obligated in any way. We hope you'll return. That simple statement spoke volumes about the "motives" for offering the new service. The message was clear: "We're glad you're here." It was a very nice touch!

Hopefully, you or a group of people in your congregation feel creatively inspired. But you're still not sure whether you're doing it right? If it feels right to you, it probably is. Unlike traditional worship, there generally aren't any right or wrong ways of doing things. Just keep in mind that the quality of an alternative service will be judged much the same as a traditional service. Pay attention to details and try to make it flow as smoothly as possible.

For a catalog of other resources on worship, hospitality, stewardship, and youth work from the publishers of this book, call 1-800-774-3360.